SEASONS OF WOMANHOOD

"This book is a real page-turner! The moving stories of nine women are very varied and the common thread of hope in Christ through their difficulties, is compelling. All who read them will be inspired and encouraged."
Fiona Castle, author and speaker

"Within the pages of this book are some remarkable stories of some remarkable women."
Di Parsons, Care for the Family

"I am delighted to be part of this book. As I look back over my own life and the lives of the other women here, I am overwhelmed by our God's supreme faithfulness and love in every circumstance."
Joanne Hogg, vocalist with Iona

"Do read this book! I promise it will inspire you, and that you'll pass it on to others. These nine very different women captured my imagination and gave my faith a real fillip. God is at work in our lives, bringing us a future and a hope."
Celia Bowring, CARE

"There are no celebrities in this book, no guaranteed happy endings, comfortable career choices or stories of star-struck success. Instead, there are real lives of real faith in a real God who shows up in the toughest of circumstances for the most ordinary of women."
Wendy Bray, writer, speaker an author

"I was deeply challenged and encouraged by the stories of these different women. Their lives speak powerfully of God's love and faithfulness through some of life's most difficult twists and turns. Jean has created a lasting gift by bringing to us, in such a readable and compelling form, the faith journeys of these courageous women."
Chris Treneer, The Navigators, Colorado Springs, CO

"These stories make it clear that Christians are not exempt from the trials and tribulations of life. The women in this book have shown their true colors of faith and courage, and have not given up on God even when there appeared to be no hope. When life threw ugly darts at them, they found a strength to navigate life with a confidence that God was there helping them with each step. This book is an inspiration—read it and be encouraged."
Kay Lucas, Executive Director, Jeff Lucas International Ministries

SEASONS OF WOMANHOOD

Stories of Despair and Hope

Jean Gibson

Authentic

MILTON KEYNES • COLORADO SPRINGS • HYDERABAD

First published in 2007 by Authentic Media
9 Holdom Avenue, Bletchley, Milton Keynes, Bucks, MK1 1QR
1820 Jet Stream Drive, Colorado Springs, CO 80921, USA
OM Authentic Media, Medchal Road, Jeedimetla Village,
Secunderabad 500 055, A.P., India
www.authenticmedia.co.uk
Authentic Media is a division of IBS-STL U.K., a company limited by
guarantee (registered charity no. 270162)

British Library Cataloguing in Publication Data

A catalogue record for this book is available from
the British Library.

ISBN-13: 978-1-86024-627-2

Cover design by David Lund
Print Management by Adare Carwin
Printed in Great Britain by J.H. Haynes and Co., Sparkford

To David

Who first helped me believe
the dream could become a reality

and in memory of
Margene
who finished well
between the writing and publication of this book

Contents

Acknowledgements

The ten women whose stories appear in this book are the reason I have been able to write it. I am deeply grateful for their willingness to share not only their lives but their secret thoughts and feelings in very personal moments. Their vulnerability has made the book what it is. My heartfelt thanks go to you all.

Jonathan Booth has been a source of encouragement and advice from the outset of the project. Your support and help have been invaluable. I have really appreciated working with Sheila Jacobs, who alongside her great literary skills has been a kind, understanding, and encouraging editor. My thanks also to a number of friends who have been willing to read chapters and offer valuable feedback. The considerate helpfulness of the whole team at Authentic has eased the path to publication of this book.

And finally, thanks to my patient husband, Brian, who has put up with a preoccupied wife, supplied cups of tea when I have been too absorbed to notice the passing of time, and stood by me through all my own seasons of womanhood.

Introduction

For the last ten years I have worked for the Christian charity Care for the Family, co-ordinating the work in Northern Ireland. Every fall we hold an event called Reality, usually in the Waterfront Hall, a wonderful concert hall in the city of Belfast, attended by almost two thousand women. More recently, hundreds of women have also attended this event in Dublin and Glasgow. It is for these women and tens of thousands like them that I have written this book—a collection of stories of women who have faced the reality of life and proved the sufficiency of God's power in many different situations. The stories cover various stages of a woman's life, from early days through to the final years. The one thing that each of these stories has in common is that they are based in the *reality* of everyday lives. Occasionally names have been changed to protect identities.

I have always been inspired by the stories of great women in the past who have overcome enormous obstacles, proving God in unusual circumstances and thereby growing stronger and more dynamic in their faith. There are other stories that are taking place around us in the twenty-first century, stories of women alive today who face life with courage and faith, sometimes doubting but desperately holding onto God and trusting even when they do not understand what is happening. They might describe their life as "ordinary"—certainly they would not think of themselves as any sort of ideal—but something in each of their lives grabbed my attention and turned my thoughts to God.

Each of the women in this book has something to teach us. They provide us with evidence that none of us is alone in our situation. It is my prayer that as you open each chapter and encounter the lives of these women you will identify with their doubts and fears, be challenged by their faith and have the courage to be "real" with God. Some of us will have faced similar situations in our own lives and yet all our paths are different because we are all different people. The good news is that God has a plan for each of us, and although we face difficulties and problems, sometimes seemingly insurmountable, there is always hope. God reaches out to us in our struggles. He has done it for others, he can do it for you!

1.

Wild Child

"Was that a little girl I saw jumping out of that first floor window?" a British soldier called to his colleague in disbelief. They were patrolling the streets of Protestant East Belfast, on the alert for anything unusual that might signal trouble. With a shout the child picked herself up and ran off laughing with her friends. "Just kids playing," muttered the soldier.

The Troubles had forced people out of their houses, which had been left empty and fallen into disrepair. These had become an adventure playground for the local children.

Elaine, the child in question, and her twin brother, were born in 1965 in the working class area of East Belfast, just as trouble between Protestants and Catholics was breaking out across Northern Ireland. Her earliest memories are of British soldiers constantly patrolling the streets where the family lived and of passing burnt-out cars on the way to school. Shops that were trading normally one day were a smoking ruin the next. As a young child growing up in that environment, Elaine accepted all this as normal.

Elaine's mother thought that the best way to prepare Elaine and her three brothers for life in this rough neighborhood was to put them out on the streets as soon as possible to "toughen them up" and learn how to survive. This they did, in Elaine's words, "by learning to break all the Ten Commandments at an early age." At five years old she was caught stealing sweets from a local shop. As she grew a little older, school attendance became intermittent. One day, Elaine with her brother and cousin sneaked into the school playground and looked through the classroom window to the amusement of their friends inside. When the headmaster appeared and asked them to come into school, they ran off with a laugh. Elaine's only thought was, "No, I don't feel like going today." To Elaine and her friends, life was a joke; all their time was spent getting into mischief and trying to escape the consequences.

Elaine's choice of friends and the decisions she made meant that her behavior was on a downward spiral from the outset. The group of eleven-year-olds of which she was a part proved their grown-up status by starting to smoke cigarettes, and a year later, by drinking alcohol. With her friends, she would stand near the local off-licence where they could get someone old enough to buy it for them. By her early teens, she was involved in solvent abuse.

The whole neighborhood was run by the Ulster Defence Association and the Ulster Volunteer Force. The latter was an organization set up in 1966 to combat what it saw as a rise in Irish nationalism by declaring war on the Irish Republican Army. The Ulster Defence Association, launched in 1971 to amalgamate the various loyalist vigilante groups, was the largest Protestant paramilitary organization in Northern Ireland. Members of these organizations ran all the youth activities in the area where Elaine lived, including the youth clubs and the discos. Far from being seen as dangerous, they took the young people camping, gave them opportunities to broaden their experience outside East Belfast, and generally befriended them. They were an everyday part of normal life in that part of the city.

For some time, Republican prisoners in Northern Ireland had been campaigning for political status and in 1980 the protest escalated when they went on hunger strike. It failed to achieve their objective. The following year, ten prisoners died during a hunger strike that lasted for seven months. By this time, Elaine was in her mid-teens, feelings were running high and her peers started joining the paramilitary groups. Once they joined one of these groups, they could never leave.

"This was nothing new to me because many of the people I knew were members of one of the terrorist organizations. The leaders of these organizations were the coolest people in the neighborhood," says Elaine. "They were the ones with the fast cars and the cool clothes. We all looked up to them and respected them. In no way did we think of them as a threat; they were our idols."

When she was sixteen, Elaine's life took a dramatic new turn when she developed a relationship with a boy who was involved in one of the loyalist organizations. Suddenly she was introduced to a whole new world on the inside of Northern Ireland terrorism. At the age of seventeen, she left home and moved into a house with her boyfriend.

"I thought I had arrived," she says. "This was the best thing that could ever happen to anybody at seventeen. I was part of this elite group, sitting drinking with them. The pubs might close at the usual time but the paramilitaries were never asked to leave, so we could sit and drink all night if we wanted to. It was so exciting it was unbelievable." Elaine was conscious of a new prestige—living in a community where there was a distinct pecking order, she had managed to jump up the ladder and find herself with new status locally through her involvement with terrorism.

This blissful existence continued for two years. Then suddenly reality hit. The police arrived one day to inform them that Elaine's partner was on a death list because of a feud between a Catholic and Protestant organization and advised them to move out of their house as soon as possible. Although they immediately acted on this advice, the change of location did not deal with the terror that now dogged Elaine every waking moment. The word "terrorist" took on a whole new meaning.

"I lived with an awful fear. We were living in a community where everybody knew everybody else, so any time I saw a stranger in the area my mind would immediately start racing and I would wonder 'Who is that? What do they want? Has he got a gun under his coat?' If I saw a strange car I would think, 'Why is it here?' I could not shake off the paranoia which now gripped me. One day we received inside information from the security forces that people from a Catholic terrorist organization were coming to get my partner. He immediately took to his heels and ran out the back door. I just sat there, lit a cigarette and thought 'What do I do?' Luckily no one came that time."

By this stage, Elaine had become very unstable emotionally, worrying and crying all the time. Drinking, which formed a large part of her normal life in any case, now increased as she regularly drank herself into oblivion in an attempt to blot out the fearful thoughts in her head.

Alcohol had been a backdrop to Elaine's life for as long as she could remember. Both her parents were regularly drunk, and from an early age Elaine was accustomed to seeing them too drunk to stand. Her mother used to tell her that her drinking problem started when Elaine and her twin brother came along. Having a toddler who was a year and four months when the twins were born meant that she really had three babies to look after. It all seemed too much to cope with and alcohol was an escape—her husband encouraged her to go out to the pub and have a break. She stopped going out when she realized she could drink more at home, not having to make her way back from the pub.

Elaine's father had a good job; both parents loved the children and in their own way tried to do their best for them. In the month of July, Protestants traditionally held marches with band parades and bonfires, often accompanied by riots in different parts of the country. Each July, Elaine's father piled the family and a tent into the back of his van and took them away camping, in order to avoid what was known locally as "the mad season." As they grew older, this was not greatly appreciated by Elaine and her brothers who always longed to get back to their friends and the excitement of the streets of Belfast.

When Elaine starting drinking as a twelve-year-old, the only pattern she had to follow was drinking to get drunk. In her early teens, her friends would often carry her home and dump her in the hallway of the house, where her parents were oblivious, too drunk themselves to notice. Social drinking, as it is usually understood, was never an option—she always tried to impress people by drinking more than them. From the time she was sixteen to the age of twenty-three, she cannot remember one Friday or Saturday night. Gradually the weekends expanded to include Thursday and Sunday nights.

One morning she came downstairs in her parents' house to find the rest of the family laughing at her. When she asked what was so funny they told her, "The police found you trying to throw yourself into the River Lagan last night and took you to the police station. When they saw the tattoo on your arm they realized who you were and brought you home."

Elaine had her boyfriend's name tattooed on her arm, a name well known to the police as he was constantly in and out of prison. She had no memory of the whole incident.

Elaine's first experience of illegal drugs came when her boyfriend encouraged her to try smoking marijuana. The first time she did it they were sitting in the sun in a park.

"It was a very funny experience," she says. "I was high, hallucinating. There was a dog coming towards us which turned into a kangaroo, then into a lion. We thought this was hilarious.

The second time was not so funny, however. This time I was in the house and it was as if the walls started breathing, moving in and out. They started to crack and blood came out of the cracks—it really freaked me out. After that I was afraid of drugs and decided to stick to alcohol. It gave me the forgetfulness that I needed without frightening me."

People around Elaine continued to do drugs but she avoided them from that point on.

One night on the way home, drunk as usual, Elaine had the strangest feeling that something was wrong. She paused at the top of her street, knew that she could not go home, and went instead to her mother's house, some distance away. In the middle of the night she woke to find the police in her bedroom to tell her that her house had been blown up. If she had continued on her way home as planned, she would have been at the door of the house when the bomb went off. Looking back now, she believes that God intervened on a number of occasions to save her from the consequences of the path she had chosen. For the next two years, Elaine lived in constant fear, wondering who had blown up her house, and when it would happen again. The story took a strange twist when she was eventually arrested for aiding and abetting the bombing of her own house. At that point she discovered that her brother had done it, claiming that he was doing her a good turn and getting rid of her old house so that she could get a new one from the Housing Executive.

Elaine's growing dependence on alcohol led from one crisis to another. Life seemed completely dark and drinking was the only relief. She had left school as soon as she could, to work in a textile factory but because of her lifestyle it became impossible for her to keep a job. On more than one occasion she was arrested for being drunk and disorderly and assaulting police officers.

One day, Elaine happened to meet her friend Pamela. She had known Pamela for years and had stayed in her house when she'd had a row with her parents and left home for the first time. She used to baby-sit for Pamela and drink together with Pamela and her husband. On this occasion, however, Elaine knew that there was something different about her friend. She was used to seeing her with a cigarette in her hand, swearing like the rest of her friends, but this day she was different—she just stood and smiled, which Elaine found somewhat unnerving. She could not work out what was going on. Pamela was running a fish and chip shop locally, and in the course of conversation made a proposition to Elaine: "Do you want to come and help out in the chippie? I need someone to give me a hand." Elaine thought about it. She was in such an unstable state that she really did not know if she could even wrap up chips or face the public. In her state of paranoia, she was afraid of the plate glass window fronting the chip shop—if anyone wanted to shoot her, it would be too easy through the glass. On the other hand, she would be working with her friend and she could also "do the double" and claim her unemployment benefit at the same time. She decided to give it a try.

Unknown to Elaine, Pamela had become a Christian and was attending a local church where Christians were praying specifically for Elaine. As a child, Elaine and her brothers had attended a Sunday school near the peace line that divided the two communities and had even been stoned on the way there. Back in those early years of her life, seeds had been planted in Elaine's heart. As she began to work alongside Pamela and see the change in her friend's life, those seeds started to germinate and grow. Pamela began to share her faith with her, the Holy Spirit started speaking to her heart and she began to question her whole way of life. In the quietness of the night she would sometimes lie awake and wonder "Why am I living like this? What is life about?"

Then events took a bizarre turn. Elaine's boyfriend, now a prominent member of his loyalist organization, used to record every news bulletin and keep cuttings from the newspaper because there were either items about him or about someone he knew. Elaine lived in fear of him, knowing that his threat to kill her if she did not co-operate was very real. He had been arrested and charged with a number of murders but managed to escape conviction through lack of evidence. One day in June 1989, they listened together to the news bulletin about the student-led demonstrations in Tiananmen Square, Beijing against the Communist Party's political repression and corruption in China. The protest was violently suppressed by armed soldiers ordered into Beijing by the government, and hundreds of people died. The picture of a lone student standing in front of army tanks, halting the progress of a column of advancing tanks for over half an hour, remained with Elaine. She had heard a prophecy somewhere that when people turned on each other the end of the world would come.

That day, she turned to her boyfriend and said, "I think the end of the world is coming."

His reply was, "It is, but don't be worrying!"

Elaine thought to herself, "I'm only twenty-three, the end of the world is coming and my life is just a mess."

Sometimes she thought about suicide in order to get out of the tangled situation she was in—it was not that she didn't love life but her world had become so complex and unhappy that she did not know where to turn. When things were bad, she cast her mind back to the stories her father used to tell them as children about his life years before in Africa, and the horrific conditions facing people there. "At least this is not as bad as Africa," was the thought she used to try to console herself.

When she went into work that day she confided in Pamela. "I think the end of the world is coming. I think I'm having a nervous breakdown."

"No, you're not. You're under conviction from God."

"Conviction? What are you talking about? What does that mean? Are you telling me I'm in trouble with God?"

"Yes. All those bad things you've been doing—one day God is going to punish you for them."

Elaine comments: "I couldn't believe it. I could just see the whole picture, because I had been in court, convicted of crimes. I knew this was bad news. I knew that as a nineteen-year-old, I had stood in front of an earthly judge, and now I realized that one day I would stand before a heavenly judge. That was the moment that the Holy Spirit opened my eyes. I knew the truth there and then—that I was guilty and deserved God's punishment. I thought there was no hope for me, and when Pamela tried to tell me that God still loved me and wanted me to have a relationship with him I had no idea what the words meant. Gradually she explained that I needed to pray and ask God for his forgiveness."

"There's one thing though," Pamela said, "you have to really mean it. When you ask God for forgiveness, you make a decision to believe that he has done it. That's what it means to put your faith in him."

At the end of that day, Elaine wandered home in a daze and climbed the stairs to her bedroom. There was normally a selection of replica machine guns, hand guns and crossbows on the wall. This day for some reason they were all on the floor and Elaine kicked them under the bed in disgust. She got down on her knees beside the weapons and called out to God: "Lord, if you are really there please come into my life. I'm so sorry for all the bad things I have done and I want you to forgive me." When she had finished praying she stood up and was immediately conscious of two things.

"The first was that Jesus Christ took away the weight of my sin. The second was that I knew I had to repent. I didn't know the word repentance at that stage but I knew immediately that I had to turn from the direction in which my life was going, turn my back on all that and live differently. That was the beginning of my Christian life—that day I entered God's kingdom. I began to feel like a child of God. I felt like a princess compared to my previous existence. I never doubted who God was or wavered in wanting to follow him and do what he wanted me to do."

As Elaine met up with her friends, she began to explain to them that she was now a Christian although she had very limited understanding of what it actually meant. When business was slack at the chip shop and they had the chance to talk, Pamela, still a new Christian herself, tried to explain to Elaine more about the Christian life. To Elaine the immediate difference seemed to be that she should stop doing things that she felt were wrong, so she decided that she would stop drinking, smoking, and cursing and that she would cut her links with the gang she was in. Her Christianity was very new and precious to her even though she understood so little. Her boyfriend thought that it was not a bad idea. Perhaps now there would be less fighting at home and instead of being out on the town, Elaine would be a model housewife, cleaning the house and having dinner ready for him when he arrived home. Elaine, too, decided that this was the Christian way to live and embarked on a much quieter lifestyle, staying at home and keeping her house as tidy as possible. As the oldest member of the gang, her friends tended to look to her to lead them so they felt lost without her. They continually pressurized her to go out with them as before but she was determined not to go back to that way of life.

As a new Christian, Elaine did not even have a Bible. Usually she had very little money but one day she had an old torn £5 note and decided that as Christians read the Bible, she should buy herself one. Greatly excited, she opened it at the beginning of the Old Testament and began to read. To her dismay, she could not make any sense of what she was reading and after a few attempts she gave up in great frustration and left the Bible to one side. Why did Christians read this? How could it ever be helpful if it was impossible to understand? She was determined to follow Christ and live as a Christian but she would have to find out how to do that without reading the Bible.

Thinking through how she should be living as a Christian, it did bother her that she had been involved in illegal activities over the years. One day she decided she would have to face her past and own up to what she had done, so, with great apprehension, she went to see a solicitor.

"I've become a Christian," she said, "and there's all this bad stuff that I have done."

After listening for a while the solicitor came over to her, put his arm round her shoulder and ushered her out of his office saying, "The police are after the big fish. You'll be okay. Don't worry about it."

Although Pamela knew that Elaine had decided to follow Christ, rather than tell her immediately all that she should do, she took things very gradually and let Elaine find her own way as a Christian. Elaine began visiting her at home and going out with her socially rather than with her former friends. Gradually Pamela's wise influence began to affect Elaine, although for months she never thought about going to church.

"I thought it was a place for good people," she says, "people who were different from me, middle-class people who were good all the time, people like missionaries, certainly not for someone like me."

Six months after making the decision to follow Christ, she realized that she was struggling and needed some direction and help in living her Christian life. Pamela suggested that perhaps Elaine should start going to church and with some trepidation, Elaine agreed to go with her. Walking in the door of the church on that first morning, she experienced severe culture shock, mirrored on the faces of those in the congregation. They saw this new arrival with her shaved head and hard face and were taken aback that she had decided to join them, despite their prayers for her.

Later, one of the ladies confessed to Elaine, "When we first saw you coming in we were afraid to look at you."

All that Elaine could think was, "This is unbelievable—all these people together, with no alcohol, no other reason to be here but the fact that they are Christians and want to meet together."

Up to that point in her life, Elaine only knew of people gathering together to drink, with a backdrop of music from a band or a disco. With the pressure of being in such a strange environment, Elaine could not lift her head to look at anyone and found it difficult and embarrassing when everyone stood to sing. She was conscious that everyone looked very clean and tidy, that men and women were there together, even with their teenage children, a situation unheard of in Elaine's usual world, where children stopped doing things with their parents as soon as possible. In this pleasant family environment, she was suddenly very conscious of her clothes, which had all come from the local charity shop. The pastor and his wife quickly assessed the situation and took these two rough new Christians under their care.

Elaine and her boyfriend began to drift apart and he realized that the relationship was going to end. At first he threatened her as to what would happen if she left him but eventually he accepted that it was over and Elaine moved back to her parents' home. Once there, she began leaving Christian tracts around the house and talking about God to anyone who would listen. The police visited the house regularly because Elaine's brothers were always in trouble, and she started witnessing to the police also. One day a policeman stopped her in the street and said, "I heard that you're a Christian. Is that right?" Word was getting out! Bemused by the change in their daughter, Elaine's parents agreed to go to church with her. A series of special meetings was taking place and they went back again and again. One night after the meeting they ended up going into two separate rooms for counseling and prayer. Some time later, they met each other at the front of the hall and announced simultaneously, "I've become a Christian!" There was great celebration in the home that evening.

A whole group of people became Christians at that time from the same neighborhood. The pastor and his wife took them to their hearts, and realizing that they were all starting from scratch, went through the main aspects of Christianity with them on a monthly basis.

"It was very basic because we knew nothing," recalls Elaine. "I was shocked when I heard that Jesus was not born on December 25. I thought that was terrible!"

Slowly, Elaine started to understand the Bible and the whole tenor of her life changed as she realized that God wanted her to go in his direction. "I just made a conscious decision to believe what the pastor said—in my world no one ever believed anything anyone said. You chose what you wanted to believe."

To this day, Elaine appreciates the willingness of the pastor and his wife to welcome her to their home, regardless of the possible effect on their teenage daughters. She was emotionally unstable, her rough life had taken its toll, but they took her in, loved her and gave her care and attention that she had never known before.

At that time, God was speaking to Elaine's brother also. Unknown to the family, he was planning to commit a serious crime, but at the same time he was struggling with the whole idea of God. One evening he looked up at the sky and prayed,

"God, if you're there and I commit this crime, it's because you have let it happen." Suddenly there was a knock at the door. The police had arrived to arrest him. In the police interrogation centre, with time to think over what had just happened, he became convinced that God was real and decided to make a commitment of his life to him.

After his decision to follow Christ, Raymond ended up spending seven and a half years in prison for his involvement in terrorism. The prison chaplain took a special interest in him and helped him to grow as a Christian during those years inside. One day, two notorious killers from the organization visited Raymond in prison to tell him that he was in serious trouble because he had told the police too much. He let them talk and then said, "Have you finished? You think you are powerful with your guns and your bombs but my God is more powerful than any of you." They stood up, shook his hand and left. Later, a friend who had also been visiting someone in prison that day said to Elaine, "There was a glow round your Raymond in the prison today." With his life completely turned around, Raymond eventually left prison with a desire to serve God in the church ministry.

Once Elaine's life changed direction, new opportunities began to open for her. She began to use the mind that she had neglected at school, picking up her education again and starting a course at Belfast Bible College. She got a job in the church, visiting those who were shut in, and when the opportunity arose to go to the Republic of Ireland for a week's mission outreach, she jumped at the chance.

Her past life continued to follow her, however. Although she had severed all links with her former associates, Elaine was now under threat from the loyalist organization she had been involved with because of her brother telling the police about his activities. When she went to the Republic, she decided to prolong her stay there, for her own safety. For Elaine, this period with Ireland Outreach was an incredible experience, as mature Christians arrived from all over the world to work in the south of Ireland. She got to know these people as friends, followed the fourteen-month training program that they were taking, and watched them live out their Christian lives. Day by day, with a growing thirst to know more, Elaine soaked up every word that was spoken.

"They gave me an all-round education," she says. "They taught me etiquette, bookkeeping, history, English, housework, how to do children's work—we even went on day trips—but above all, they taught me spiritually. God just transformed me."

Elaine thrived in this fertile environment. She appreciated the sense of loving authority that she found in the leadership, because in all her young life she had never known any authority apart from terrorism, and now she reveled in the security that it gave. God's Word became her ultimate authority. As she started to read the Bible in a version that she could understand, and learned how to apply it to her life, she began to realize the power that it had to change her.

One day, a tall, handsome stranger arrived from the United States to set up a computer system for Ireland Outreach. He and Elaine became firm friends as she neared the end of her time in the Republic of Ireland. On her return to Belfast, Woody wrote explaining that his feelings for her were more than friendship. Elaine wrote back giving a list of reasons why the relationship would never work—he was American, cultured, well-educated, from a totally different lifestyle and background. He responded to each of her doubts with an answer from the Bible, explaining how it could work.

Elaine, dumbfounded by his persistence, confided in her mother, who said, "If I were you, I would give it a go."

Elaine's parents had met Woody and felt that he was a reliable young man who would be good for their daughter. Elaine saw him only as a gentleman and a good friend but gradually her feelings blossomed into something deeper. "I have learned so much from Woody," she says. "From the day and hour he met me he treated me like a lady."

However, she was very conscious of his wealthy background, and in particular of his well-educated mother who had devoted her life to the all-round development of her young son. Woody had grown up near Washington DC going to art galleries and the theatre. He'd spent his summers at his grandfather's lakeside house in the State of New Jersey where he'd enjoyed the wonderful outdoor life and many happy hours canoeing on the lake. It was a life as different as it was possible to be to Elaine's. It was not a life unmarked by suffering, however, as his dearly loved mother died when he was a young teenager, leaving Woody with some understanding of Elaine's low times.

"I got the bargain of a lifetime," says Elaine. "He swept me off my feet and took me to America to live. He took the first six months off work and took me on a tour round his relatives. His family were academically gifted—one aunt was a reporter, another was a doctor—and the family were all lovely Christians. It was a whole new world and I was overwhelmed. It was like being in heaven."

Woody started to work for Washington Bible College as their computer manager and Elaine, to her joy and amazement, began to read a theology course. She came across a radio program from the Christian organization Focus on the Family and was very impressed with the work Dr Dobson was doing among families across the United States. He became a role model and a strong influence in her life as a wife, and eventually as a mother, when her first baby girl was born. She attended ladies' Bible studies, where the women memorized verses of Scripture and challenged each other to live for God. These young mothers did not conform to any of the stereotypes that Elaine had of Christians but they talked openly about their Christianity and lived it out daily in their families. Between the teaching she was receiving at church and college and through listening to Christian radio, Elaine's Christian life grew and blossomed during those four years in the United States.

Together, Elaine and Woody found that they were befriending people who had problems with drugs and alcohol. They were familiar with the organization Stauros (from the Greek word meaning 'cross'), an organization started in Scotland by someone who was himself a recovering alcoholic and wanted to reach out to others suffering from addiction. Elaine's mother had been helped by Stauros in the early days after she became a Christian and Elaine and Woody were impressed by the work they did. They invited some people from Stauros to come to their home in Baltimore, and after meetings with them, knew that God was calling them into this ministry. When the idea was first broached by the people from Stauros, Elaine's response was negative. She did not want to be constantly involved with and surrounded by people like this again. She had reached America, she had a new life, she had arrived and she did not want to go back into the atmosphere of her former life.

"I didn't mind doing God's work when it suited me," she says "But I didn't want to leave my new life to be involved with all the pain of the addict's world. Then God spoke to me one day and changed my heart. He said, 'It's not your work, it's my work. I'm the One who heals the addict. You are only the vessel and the spokesperson. Yours may be the feet, and hands, and mouth that I use but it is my supernatural power that changes the addict.' I fell in love with the ministry to addicts after that. It became my passion to introduce them to the supernatural healer."

Woody and Elaine returned to Northern Ireland where they now work with Stauros. Elaine says with a rueful smile, "When we went to America, Woody took me on a tour of the States to meet his family. When we returned to Ireland, I took him to the prison to meet mine." Woody, however, loves Ireland and their life together now. They have a happy family that is the opposite of everything that Elaine knew as a child.

"We used to play pubs as children, selling alcohol and cigarettes to each other. Now my children play church—one plays the piano, one preaches, and they all sing together."

The verses that meant the most to Elaine when she first came to Christ are Matthew 11:28–30: "Come to me, all you who are weary and burdened, and I will give you rest. Take my yoke upon you and learn from me, for I am gentle and humble in heart, and you will find rest for your souls. For my yoke is easy and my burden is light." Those words were very precious to her in the early days when she did not understand much about the Bible or what it meant, but she knew she needed rest from the fear that dogged her.

"The message that came to me all those years ago when I was so broken is still the same. God still takes broken vessels and makes them into something beautiful. He can do abundantly above what we can ask or think when we surrender everything to him. For the first year and a half after I became a Christian, I could not sleep and I had nightmares because of the anxiety with which I struggled. I did not fall into the alcohol-induced stupor that I was used to and I really felt there was a supernatural battle going on for my mind. I had been so tormented and psychologically damaged during my time with the paramilitaries that sometimes I didn't know whether things were really happening or whether it was all in my imagination. I just kept repeating 'The blood of Jesus Christ' as a protection and the things that I was seeing would vanish. I used to have a particularly bad night after I shared my testimony with others. But the past does not hurt me any more now. The nightmares gradually disappeared. My focus is on Christ rather than on the past."

Elaine's brothers are married with families of their own. As young people, terrorism used to be their only after-school activity and alcohol was their common bond. The whole topic of conversation was about who had been arrested, who had been beaten up and who was going to get beaten up. Elaine was the first in her whole extended family to become a Christian and to leave Belfast. As more of the family became Christians, they discovered that their bond in Christ drew them closer to each other.

"We have great fun together now," Elaine says. "We don't need alcohol to have a laugh together. We share all kinds of things with each other. Our relationships are totally transformed."

Elaine's life has changed completely since she handed it over to God. These days when she goes back to East Belfast, she meets some of the friends she once knew there. Often they do not recognize her until she introduces herself because she has changed outwardly as well as inwardly. At forty years of age, Elaine has now been accepted by Queens University Belfast where she plans to study mental health in preparation for the work that she believes God has for her. Contrary to her own natural inclinations, he has given her a heart for people suffering from the effects of drugs and alcohol and for those in prison.

"God wants us to fulfill our potential. He has many exciting plans for us in the future—we just need to keep following him and trusting him to lead us." She is often invited to speak publicly about her experiences, which she is happy to do if it highlights what God can do in a life. Recently she started a prayer group for mothers of children in the local primary school.

"Jesus Christ is the greatest thing," she says. "We need to let our children know how exciting it is to follow him. It's not just about going to church on Sunday."

In Lewis Carroll's children's classic, *Alice in Wonderland*,[1] Alice comes to a fork in the road and asks the Cheshire Cat which direction she should take. The Cat replies that it depends very much on where she'd like to go, to which Alice answers that she doesn't care much. In that case the Cat's verdict is that it doesn't matter which way she goes. If we don't care where we are going, any road will do. The direction of the rest of our lives is decided at the fork in the road. As a young woman, Elaine chose to follow Christ and has seen him transform her life in an amazing way. If we choose to follow his direction, we too will know the wonder of walking that road with him, living a life of excitement and purpose at which we can only guess as we set out.

**No eye has seen,
no ear has heard,
no mind has conceived
what God has prepared for those
who love him
1 Corinthians 2:9**

2.

Nothing but the Best

"Let's go for a walk after church on Sunday."

Wandering round the harbor on a Sunday evening seemed a pleasant enough prospect to Margaret, especially with Gareth, whom she had known for years and whose company she enjoyed. She had a wide circle of friends, both boys and girls, who went out together for the evening after choir practice or into a nearby seaside town on a Saturday or Sunday night. It was all lighthearted fun. Gareth was part of the crowd at church and shared her Christian faith and concern for others. At the age of seventeen, to have a boyfriend aged twenty-four was quite a status symbol, and although such thoughts were far from Margaret's mind, other people thought he would make a great husband. He was steady, intelligent, and good-looking, he came from a Christian family; what more could one ask? Like other girls, Margaret looked forward to one day finding someone special, getting married and having a family—six children might be about right, she thought.

However, Gareth was not "the one." No matter how perfect everyone else thought he was for her, she could not see them having a long-term future together. Besides, she had an innate sense that her future lay further afield. She had a broader vision for her life than raising a family locally in quiet domesticity. Something about that picture did not fit with who she was. An inner restlessness told her that there was a whole world to explore outside the rural environment where she had grown up.

Margaret knew that the relationship was becoming more meaningful to Gareth than it was to her. It was difficult to know what to do about it, however, without hurting him or losing his friendship. She said nothing, allowing things to continue as usual but feeling increasingly uncomfortable. On her birthday she received a card, covered in yellow roses, with a romantic greeting on the front. It was the kind of card that might have sent any girl into ecstatic delight. Margaret took one look at it and burst into tears. This had all got out of hand. How was she going to explain her feelings to this kind and considerate friend whom she respected but did not love? She began to worry. Was there something odd about her that she did not appreciate a good relationship that seemed so right to everyone else? Yet she knew that there was more that she needed to find out about life, about who she was and what God wanted her to be. She was intrigued about what the future held, always reaching beyond the present situation. Somehow she felt that God's plan for her life was bigger than Gareth and her home town. Reluctantly, she gathered up all her courage and tried as best she could to explain her feelings to a somewhat confused young man.

Margaret's family lived in a quiet fishing town on the east coast of Northern Ireland. Along with her brother, she enjoyed the security of a loving, stable home where Christian parents prayed for and with them from their early days and encouraged them to develop all their abilities and interests as they grew up. She knew that they loved her and were proud of her and was conscious of the strength that gave her as a young person. Her parents were steady, sensible, and wise, setting a framework and boundaries that gave her a sense of security and well-being. That stability was to be the basis of her life, building her self-esteem and giving her the confidence to choose and follow God's way for her.

As soon as she arrived at teacher training college in Belfast, Margaret realized that she was a city girl at heart. She embraced all that was offered at college and in the city, rejoiced in the chance to broaden her horizons and flourished in the stimulation of the cultural and academic opportunities that opened up for her. She made many good friends at college and met a number of very suitable young men but did not allow herself to get caught up in a relationship that was not right for her. She did not want any more complicated situations.

After qualifying as a teacher, much as she loved Belfast, Margaret decided to accept a teaching opportunity back in her home town. She worked happily in the High School for a few years and helped out in her local church. She was always busy, interested in others and helping where she could. Brought up in a home where her parents concentrated on their work and on helping the community, her focus tended to be outward rather than on herself. She became very involved in whatever project was on hand, not leaving much time to worry about not having a boyfriend or husband. Life was about doing what God wanted her to do. She was happy in the anticipation that God would open up the possibility of marriage at some stage in the future. Sometimes she did wonder why she was not finding the right partner and she certainly had her dreams of what that would entail but she knew that she wanted God's will more than her own so she was prepared to wait.

Margaret's parents, especially her mother, would have liked her to get married but they refused to pressurize her. If her mother ever passed any remark about it, her father would respond, "Oh, she's fine the way she is." He was quite happy to have his beloved daughter living at home. Sometimes, however, it was difficult for Margaret to face the expectations of others in a community where the normal pattern was to get married and have children. Regularly people would say to her, "I can't understand why you're not married." This remark Margaret learned to deal with over the years, continuing to hear it throughout her life.

"Even yet they haven't given up!" she says with a laugh.

A few transient boyfriends came and went but none were right. Everyone expected her to marry—but they decided that she was "hard to please." After teaching for a few years in her home town, she became restless and felt that God was calling her to do something different with her life in terms of Christian service. She had a talk with her church minister, whose opinion she greatly respected, and decided to move out into the unknown by applying to London Bible College. She was both excited and apprehensive about this new phase in her life. She did not know what God wanted her to do afterwards but she was open to follow his leading wherever that took her.

As soon as people heard that she was going to Bible College there was a united response: "Ah, you're bound to meet someone there. Think of all those fine young Christian men!"

Margaret was really unhappy with this. It was against the whole focus of her thinking. She wanted to do what God wanted and discover his plan for her life. Her aim was to go and learn; to have a rich, enjoyable time of study without the pressure of looking at every male as a possible husband.

At that time, a minister and his wife who had met at London Bible College came to live in the area and this added fuel to the fire as far as others were concerned.

"Robert and his wife met each other there. You're bound to meet someone, Margaret."

Margaret bit her tongue. She was very conscious that this was not the mindset she wanted to have as she went to Bible College. She wanted to be free to enjoy the company of everyone she would meet and to learn from a new experience without emotional complications.

It was at this point that she read a book called *Take My Life* by Michael Griffiths.[2] She found this one of the most challenging books she had ever read. It went through every phrase of what was sometimes called the "consecration hymn," by Frances Ridley Havergal (1836–79). "Take my Time," "Take my Silver and my Gold," "Take my Intellect," and then a chapter entitled "Take my Love." At the end of each chapter of that book there was a series of questions, and as she asked herself those questions, Margaret realized this was something that she needed to sort out: Was she willing to be single for the rest of her life if that was what God was asking of her? Was she willing for whatever God had in store for her? Was she really willing for anything? This was the most painful point in her life so far, as she faced up to the fact that she might never marry and visualized living the rest of her life alone.

"As I read this, I knew that I had to honestly face the possibility that the Lord might choose that I should remain single. The reality of the prospect of lifelong singleness was hard. It went against all my natural desires and against the cultural norms of the community in which I had been brought up. I thought, prayed, and wept my way through this for several weeks until I came to the point where I was honestly able to say, 'Lord, if that is your will for me then I know it will be best. Please give me the grace to accept it.' It was not easy—it was a very real challenge in all sorts of ways—but the Lord did give me the grace to accept it and to learn to live happily with it."

She says, "I didn't choose to be single. I didn't at that point want to be single but I chose to be willing to be whatever God had in his plan for me and to do whatever God wanted me to do, even if that meant I would remain single for the rest of my life. I told God I would do it if that was his will and if he would give me the grace to cope with the situation. I made a commitment to go God's way in the whole matter."

That commitment was a very freeing experience for Margaret. It meant that she was able to go to Bible College unburdened by the expectations of others or the desires of her own heart in relation to men. She watched others at Bible College struggle as they worked through these issues for themselves and she ended up talking and praying with some of them as they came to terms with what it might mean for them. She also, as forecast by her friends, met some very interesting and attractive men at Bible College. She never wanted to play down her femininity or the fact that she was a woman and she took it as a good and normal thing to be attracted to someone of the opposite sex, but none of the friendships with the men she met there developed into anything more. She felt free to be herself and enjoy the company of everyone around her in that very special experience at Bible College. She reveled in the stimulation of biblical and theological study, Christian fellowship, and spiritual growth.

Leaving Bible College, Margaret became a staff worker with the Universities and Colleges Christian Fellowship for five years. She had the distinction of being the first woman traveling secretary for the International Fellowship of Evangelical Students in Ireland. She was also the first traveling secretary to live in Dublin, where she began to build on the pioneering work begun sporadically by others. She traveled throughout Ireland, loving it, working with these young people who were at a very formative stage in their lives, having the privilege of listening to them, praying with them, encouraging them. She helped many of them through their relationship difficulties, with a quiet chuckle at what she saw as God's sense of humor. She made great friendships in those years, some of which remain to this day.

Margaret had always loved children and the thought that she might never have children of her own was one of the hardest parts of being single. While she was preparing to go to Bible College, one of her friends was preparing to get married. A few years later Margaret visited her when this friend had a little two-year-old girl.

"She was beautiful," says Margaret. "She was like a little doll. She sat on my knee while we listened to a tape of children's songs. She was so bright and musical and able to catch the tunes of the songs. A great sense of sadness came over me. She was so lovely and I realized that I would probably never have a little girl like this."

It was a realization that her singleness was in a sense a double bereavement—the loss of children as well as the loss of a partner. Her acceptance of God's will did not mean that life would be without times of struggle or sadness.

Margaret has learned to "rejoice with those who rejoice," having attended many weddings over the years. She enjoyed every one of them and has wonderful friendships with her married friends. They have drawn her into the circle of their married life—and she has had much joy in knowing and loving their children. Accepted as part of the family, she has been able to love the children and look after them, take them out on trips and enjoy their company. As things have turned out, she has had many children in her life and feels that in the end she has not missed out. She takes special pleasure in her two fabulous nieces who have brought such joy and fun into her life. She finds it sad when she talks to others who are single who do not want to go to social occasions or events with married people because they fear the conversation will be all about children and family.

"I am around children and young people so much that I am very happy to talk about them," she says. "That doesn't bother me because I have always been used to working with friends' and cousins' children. I love being with them and talking about them. It's a privilege and joy to do that."

One friend says, "We love to see Margaret arriving because in five minutes she has the children organized and away out for a walk and they all have a great time while I get peace to get on with things at home."

Margaret's version of it is, "I feel as if I have had hundreds of children, through my career in teaching, through church, through Sunday school, through youth groups, through the student work, through friends and family."

Margaret does not allow herself to dwell on any sense of loss for long. She prayed a great deal that God would give her a grateful heart for all the blessings that she enjoys and she feels that God answered that prayer, helping her to put the singleness issue in the context of all the other lovely things in her life. She was always conscious that she had good parents and a great family and that marriage and children of her own was only one part of a whole life.

Isaiah chapter 54 is a Bible passage that has been particularly meaningful to her:

> "… more are the children of
>   the desolate woman
>   than of her who has a husband,"
>   says the LORD …
> All your sons will be taught by the LORD,
>   and great will be your children's
>   peace.
>   Isaiah 54:1,13

She feels that this has been truly fulfilled in her life. The second verse of this chapter goes on to say "lengthen your cords, [and] strengthen your stakes" and Margaret sees a connection between the two verses. Unencumbered by husband and family, she has been free in a different way to strengthen her stakes in God and lengthen her cords in his service. There are things she has been able to do as a single person that she could not have done if she had been married. She has been free to minister to people, to sit with them and pray with them when they needed it and were going through a very difficult time.

"I was free—I did not have to worry about getting home because others were waiting for me. There is a real freedom in being able to do those things without having to worry about time or other commitments. There are so many hurting people who need someone to sit alongside them maybe for a month or two, maybe for a year, to help them through a rough patch. Can you do anything better than give someone a secure base from which they can move on in life again? That is a privilege."

Margaret acknowledges, however, that to be single and celibate in Britain is to live against the cultural norm.

"Young people today are subjected to much more pressure from the media, with magazines, television programs, and films all giving the message that sex is all-important and no one is complete without a partner."

As a young person, she was conscious of a certain pressure from those around her but not the relentless power of the constant media messages today. It helped that she was an independent thinker—she describes herself as stubborn-minded—and always wanted to be true to herself rather than fitting in with the crowd or doing what others did. It was not that she particularly wanted to be different from others, but she always wanted to be herself.

She sees sex as only part of life and only part of marriage. Modern media has elevated its importance in our society but in reality it is only a part of the greater whole. She accepts that as a single woman she has feelings and needs that are not being met but she also accepts that she was not given the gift of marriage so therefore sexual experience is not going to be part of her life.

"Over the years I have come to terms with sexual abstinence—that is God's standard for the unmarried and I have always accepted that. I am, however, very much a female with all that means and I still feel the chemistry of an attractive male! I take that as a positive thing and I enjoy my femininity. I have been able to express that in my life through clothes, interests, creative pursuits, and good friendships with both men and women. I have been blessed with many male friends of all ages who have affirmed me as a woman and offered me their friendship in a genuine and non-threatening way."

In her teens and twenties the question of sex was more of an issue for her and sometimes she wondered if she was not attractive to men or did not have the sexual appeal they were looking for. She worried that she was the kind of person that no one wanted to marry. Why would they not choose her? What was wrong with her? For a while it threatened her self-esteem as a young person but fortunately she was surrounded by the affirmation of family and friends who carried her through that stage. Looking back now she accepts that if she had really wanted to marry someone, the opportunities were there. She made deliberate choices in certain situations, believing that particular relationships were not right for her at that time.

People would say to her, "You're too hard to please." Sometimes she would wonder about this.

"Am I too hard to please? Should I lower my standards in what I am looking for in a relationship? Am I too arrogant?"

Her church minister had seen too many wrong choices. "Just continue to be hard to please," he said, "because sometimes people don't make the best choices and end up marrying the first man who comes along."

Years later she laughingly said to him, "It's all your fault. You told me to be hard to please!"

Regardless of other people's opinions, Margaret was not prepared to marry and settle down with anybody for the sake of it. She always felt that it would have to feel right and she would have to know that it was God-ordained. She knew that God wanted only the very best for her life. She has had her painful moments, having fallen for one or two attractive and wonderful men over the years. A couple of times she has thought, "Now, there is someone I could really respect, work in partnership with, and enjoy sharing life with." Having prayed about it, however, and subsequently not seen anything develop out of those relationships, she had to come to the difficult acceptance that this was not in God's plan for her.

"Not only do you lose the person you had hopes for but it underlines the fact that you might not get married at all. It was not easy to accept that there was no future. But the Lord gave me what I needed to retain their friendship and receive from the richness of that without threatening them with romantic ideas that were not right for either of us. These were lessons in patience and trust, self-control, and obedience. I am grateful for having known them—but also very glad that I did not make the wrong choices."

Those gentlemen remain good friends and are married now to other people.

Margaret discovered that there came a point of acceptance in the end, and in that acceptance, the road to freedom. She was able to embrace where she was in life and enjoy that. She was reassured that she was a normal human being when she felt drawn to a man so even when it did not work out she accepted that it was all part of the human experience.

"I am so grateful to God for giving me what I need to live as a single person and to be happy with it. I don't see myself as less of a person just because I'm not married. I'm a whole person because that's the way God made me. I would love young girls to grasp this and not feel they are less in some way because they do not have a man in their life. That is a lie. You are a whole complete wonderful person whom God has made. You are created for relationship but we live in a fallen world. There isn't necessarily someone for everyone and some of us are called to be single. It is a shame when we get into a really unhappy place about it because it can spoil our whole life if we let it. People can make some terrible mistakes because they are desperate to get married. From thirty to thirty-five can be a particular danger zone as people feel they are running out of time and the temptation is to settle for second best. It is better to be single than in a marriage that is not the best."

When she finished her time with UCCF, Margaret returned to teach in Belfast. In 1985, her father died—the father who had cherished and encouraged her for as long as she could remember. She then took responsibility for her mother until her death in 1997 and during those twelve years they built a home together in Belfast. One of the things that took her by surprise, in addition to a deep sense of loss at the death of her parents, was a rare feeling of aloneness. The sense of isolation was even more profound with the loss of her mother as she realized there was no one left who had known her always. From a human point of view, those who had given her total security from childhood had gone—it was a strange feeling and one that took a while to fade. However, her overriding feeling was one of deep gratitude for all that she had been given in two very special parents. She had a rich fund of happy memories and the love and support of her brother and his family.

Two years after her mother's death, Margaret moved to London, a city with which she has always had a special affinity. In a demanding post heading up a London-based charity, she looks back now on a very full and satisfying life as a single person. Over the years she has faced up to the various aspects of married life that she has missed, and taking it all in balance, accepts that God's plan for her life has been the best.

"Several things helped me:

- The growing understanding that God loved me far more than I could ever know, that I was very precious to him, a unique individual, and he would only do what was best for me.
- That the Lord knew me better than I knew myself and his will would be the absolute best for me—it would 'fit' me exactly. If I had entered into any of those relationships that were possible when I was in my teens and twenties I would have felt trapped in them. I believe that I was meant to be somewhere else; I was meant to have a different kind of life.
- That the Lord had plans for my life and that he would fulfill them if I walked in obedience to him.
- That singleness was a gift, just as marriage was a gift, and would leave me free to do things that I could not do if I was married—this has certainly proved true for me. I was able to take opportunities that I could not have taken as a married person. I know what Paul meant when he said that a single person can devote herself to the work of God. I am free to do what God wants me to do without the restrictions and responsibilities of home and family. I did have responsibilities to my parents but to a large extent I am a free agent with my own individuality and I enjoy the benefits of that.

Really understanding those facts in the depths of your heart can make a huge difference in your attitude. These are the absolute truth. Anything that society tells us that is different from that is not truth. These are the principles that have undergirded my thinking about myself and singleness all through the years. Of course, I have made mistakes and I've had my moments of sadness and disappointment. I acknowledge that it is entirely by God's grace that I have lived at peace with being single and that I can now rejoice in it as being the very best for me."

In recent years she has done some of the current personality profiles and tests to do with gifting and some of these show clearly that she has the gift of celibacy. She accepts this with a smile. She underlines the fact that she would never choose to be single but what she does choose is to go God's way. Because singleness has been part of his plan, she has deliberately chosen to accept it positively and gratefully. As the years have passed she has seen some of the sadness experienced by friends and acquaintances through unhappy marriages and broken relationships and has come to realize that marriage does not solve problems, but raises different ones. She says today that she has no regrets.

"I thank him that I am at peace with myself and who I am in Christ. He walks with me through every day. Years ago we used to sing a song, "He is my everything". You can sing that pretty glibly but I used to think about it in the context of being single. I can truly say today that he is my everything and he has been my all. I have found him to be friend, brother, father, husband, guide—everything. He is the one who holds my hand, puts his arm around me, holds me close, tells me he loves me, gives me comfort, brings me joy. That is my experience and it is entirely of his grace and love."

Margaret has a special ministry with those who find it hard to be single. She tries to help and support them in their pain and be an encouragement to them. She has also seen some interesting answers to prayer on behalf of her single friends, because although it has not been God's will for her, she believes strongly in marriage and has prayed for many to find husbands. One particular friend could not cope with the idea of being single and she and Margaret agreed to pray together that God would provide a husband for her. She moved from one place of work to another, not really very happy about the move and as she moved Margaret said to her, "Well, we've been praying together over the years. You never know what might be round the corner in this new situation!" Sure enough, a short time later she met the man who became her husband. God answered that particular prayer by providing a husband while for Margaret, he answered by giving the grace to live singly.

Margaret comments, "It is not a case of it being better to be married or single but rather a case of what is right for each person, what God's will is for us."

She still lives with an open mind on the matter and still finds men attractive—which her niece now finds very amusing.

"Who knows what will happen? Life isn't over yet! I'm very happy, very content, totally satisfied, never lonely and I do praise God for that. I am so grateful that he has allowed me to enjoy my life and to enjoy the people he has brought into my life, whether they are male or female. At this stage of my life as I look back I feel privileged to be single. I am so grateful for the rich and satisfying life the Lord has given me—I could not ask for more."

Friends have been a very important part of Margaret's life. She has taken time to cultivate friendships and has many friends of all kinds, male, female, married, and single. She refuses to think of herself specifically as a single person. Sometimes when people invite her to dinner parties, it turns out that she is the only single person. It never even occurs to her or her hosts that there is any problem. She has been invited as a friend and there is no pressure to have another person there to balance the numbers. It is not really an issue. Perhaps that is because Margaret herself takes it so much in her stride.

"For me it is about being interested in other people. If my married friends want to talk about their children, that is great. There would be something wrong if I could not talk about them because that is part of their life and I need to be able to talk about them. I have had such lovely experiences as a result of being involved in the life of my friends and their children."

Margaret acts as a kind of godmother, for example, to three young people, children of a Belfast friend. She has watched them grow up from babies to their current student status. These days they text her if they are coming to London, and make use of her apartment to leave their bags or perhaps stay overnight. If one of them is playing at a concert, Margaret will go along to hear them in lieu of parents. She treasures the relationship and says, "It's lovely. God has been enormously good."

Margaret's overriding conviction, borne out by her life experience, is that the God who loves her wants nothing but the best for her. She is content to allow him to work that out in her life.

"My journey with singleness has not been without its pain and heartache. I do not pretend that singleness is an easy option. In spite of that, I have no regrets as I look back. The Lord's love has never failed me—and it has all been wonderfully worthwhile.

"All I would say is to concentrate on what God says about you as a unique and precious individual. Focus on his love for you and the fact that he has a purpose for your life. As you immerse yourself in his love and follow his will you will discover that the most surprising and beautiful things will happen. Marriage may well be part of God's plan for you—but what is more important is to make the most of the present in every way so that you are a fulfilled, satisfied, and interesting person—prepared for a rich relationship with the partner God may have chosen for you.

"Do not live in the future when it might happen—live fully in today and tomorrow will take care of itself. The future is in God's hands and there are no more loving or capable hands than his."

**Not one of all the good promises
the LORD your God gave you has failed.
Joshua 23:14**

3.

The Long Wait

"I've had enough of this. Your whole life revolves around that church. You have to make a decision now—it's either me or God."

Pamela stared in horror as her husband delivered the ultimatum. She had just come in from a meeting at church to find him waiting for her. How had it come to this? She knew he hated her being at church events but for him to ask her to choose between him and her faith—that was taking it a step too far. She took a deep breath.

"I cannot turn my back on God. If I have to choose between you and him, then it will have to be him."

"Then that's your choice," said John as he left the house, closing the door behind him.

Pamela knew he meant it. Ever since she had become a Christian their relationship had been in a downward spiral as John became more and more resentful of the time she spent at church. Her desire to read the Bible, pray, and spend time with other Christians meant that she had a new focus outside her home and apart from her husband. She knew that John felt he had been left behind as an unnecessary part of her exciting new world. If only he would become a Christian too. That would resolve the problem and they could enjoy the Christian life together. Why did God not answer her prayers for him?

To the casual acquaintance Pamela was a happy, confident, and successful woman. When she was just four years old, her mother had died of a heart attack, and as a lone parent her bereaved father put his best efforts into bringing up his little daughter and her two brothers. He set strict boundaries for them and sent them to Sunday school and church. As she grew older, Pamela was confirmed in the Church of Ireland and always had a deep fear of God although she had no idea that she could have any kind of personal relationship with him.

Pamela's occasional visits to church with her aunt and uncle suddenly became much more interesting on the day she noticed a handsome blue-eyed boy in the choir. Two years later that blue-eyed boy became her husband. They were blissfully happy, planning the wedding and setting up home together. As Pamela got to know her husband's family, she realized that Bible reading and prayer played an important part in that home, a concept which she could not quite grasp. She had always lived what she considered to be a good life because she had great respect for her father and never wanted to do anything that would bring shame or disgrace on her family, but this idea of reading the Bible and praying outside of church was new to her.

Attending her husband's church with him, she heard people talk about a relationship with God, a phrase she had not come across before and could not understand. She watched one particular older lady, sensing a depth of spirituality that she admired and eventually came to want for herself. The more she got to know people there, the more she began to realize that her heart was hungry for something which she could not put into words. When a special two-week outreach event was held in the church, she attended regularly, and on the final night drove thoughtfully back down the country lane that led to their home. She parked the car, walked straight into the house and announced, "John, I want to get right with God."

John had grown up in a Christian home and knew exactly what she was talking about. His response was clear and immediate: "You can do whatever you want but don't involve me."

Pamela knew that John wanted nothing to do with Christianity in any personal sense, although he had been a regular church attender all his life. She also knew, however, that she had to sort out her own relationship with God, regardless of John's position. That night she asked God for forgiveness of her past and committed her life completely to him. It was a decision that she never regretted, despite all that happened later.

The next morning was the start of a new week. John's parents lived a hundred yards along the road from the young couple and looked after their little two-year-old granddaughter while Pamela was at work. Pamela could not wait to get to their house the next morning to tell them her news. As she had anticipated, they were overjoyed at this answer to their prayers. As she drove away, their words re-echoed in her mind, "John will come too." They would pray for him together now. Over the next few years, much of the support and nurturing of Pamela's early Christian faith came from John's parents.

John and Pamela had been married for four years when Pamela made her momentous decision. As she began to grow as a Christian, however, her husband started to rebel. He could not understand that she could still love him as her husband while talking about a love for God which irritated him. Gradually his resentment grew as Pamela's commitment to Christ became a barrier between them. The atmosphere in the home changed imperceptibly until hostility and antagonism completely replaced the love they had once known. Pamela came home from meetings where she had been worshipping God, with her heart full of joy and praise, only to be confronted with ill-feeling and animosity. John had become consumed with a hatred of everything to do with Christianity. He would sneer at God and demean her love for him.

By this stage there were three little children in the home. As a young Christian, Pamela did not really think about sharing her faith with her children. Not having grown up in a Christian home, it never occurred to her to talk to them much about God or to pray with them when they were little. She thought they could not possibly understand. She did, however, want them to go to Sunday school and fortunately on this John agreed with her. Coming from a Christian home, he felt that it was the done thing for all children and a necessary part of their education. Later, as the children began to grow up through primary school, Pamela could see them growing up as she had done, knowing about God but not really knowing him personally. That was when she began to pray in earnest for them. John still went to church on a Sunday morning, so in some ways it did not appear to the children that there was much difference between their parents. In an attempt to shield them from the discord, John and Pamela tried to make sure that the arguments and disagreements about Pamela's Christian life happened when the children were in bed or out of the house.

One day, Pamela could not find a worship tape that she particularly liked. She loved to listen to it as she worked in the kitchen and knew it had been on the kitchen counter the day before. After a fruitless search she gave up in frustration and decided to listen to the recording of a service that someone had given her. When she went to look for it, however, it also was missing. What was going on? How could she misplace both tapes? She began to check through her collection and discovered that a number of her Christian tapes were not there. A suspicion began to grow in her mind as she donned rubber gloves and began to go through the rubbish bin. In among the potato peelings and food wrappings, she discovered her precious tapes. John was the only one who could have done this. Among the rubbish she also discovered torn up scraps of paper containing notes about a passage of Scripture that was particularly precious to her. He had destroyed these things that meant so much to her but symbolized the enemy to him. The thought of it shook her to the core. How could she bear to go on living in this atmosphere where all that she loved most only stirred up hurt and anger?

The older lady at church whose life had first impressed Pamela was a constant source of encouragement to her now. As they met to pray together, Pamela understood the value of Christian support in her situation.

"I thought that if God had helped her cope through all the peaks and troughs of her life over the years, then God would see me through also. It helped me hold on to God when things were at their most difficult."

The battles about Christianity continued for years and gradually Pamela was worn down by the constant hostility. As time went on, she realized that her marriage was coming to an end. She struggled with her husband and she struggled with God. She said to God, "Surely you have the power to bring my husband to know you as his Savior." God gave her an answer that became very precious to her: "Be still, and know that I am God" (Ps. 46:10).

Sometimes, lying in bed at night, crying into her pillow while her husband was sleeping, Pamela pleaded with God: "Lord, how can I be still when such turmoil is going on in our home?" When things between them got particularly bad, John would walk out. Pamela was terrified that he would leave for good and yet underneath the fear was the awareness that God was still in control. "I started praying that God would give me such a love for my husband that no matter what he would say, no matter what he would do, he couldn't pierce my heart." She prayed that God would always remind her of the verse he had given her. At times, no matter where she was, she would stand still and repeat it to herself. When she was crying from pain and frustration she would take a deep breath, force herself to stop and say, "Be still."

During these years, Pamela had been working in a fashion store in the town where they lived and for some time had felt that she would like to have her own fashion business. Eventually that dream became a reality when she and John took the plunge and opened their own shop in the town. They did the buying together but Pamela did the main running of the business while John continued in his job locally with British Telecom. Pamela flourished in the challenge of seeing the business grow, and the long hours of work seemed insignificant in the satisfaction of seeing it well established.

One Monday morning, John was getting ready to go out to work at his usual time, as the children clattered down the stairs for breakfast. He normally set off for work long before everyone else left the house but Pamela noticed that he had disappeared without coming in to say goodbye to them all. She even commented to her eldest daughter at the breakfast table, "That's very strange. It's not like your dad to go off to work without saying goodbye."

About three quarters of an hour later, the doorbell rang and Pamela opened it to find a policeman standing awkwardly on the doorstep. Pamela knew instantly that something was badly wrong.

"Mrs Forrest?" he said. "Can I come in?"

Numbly Pamela showed him into the living room. Hesitating a little, he told her that John had been taken from the house by two armed men while she was getting breakfast ready for the children. They had forced him to drive to the shop and open up the premises so that they could pour inflammable liquid round it and set it alight. They then drove John out along a lonely country road. At one point they put a gun to his head but at the last minute they seemed to change their mind and instead locked him in the boot of his car, threw the car keys over the hedge, and drove away in another vehicle. With the strength of desperation John was able to break out of the car and raise the alarm but by this time the shop was well alight.

Pamela was stunned. Incidents like this were happening to businesses all over the country during the Troubles but she had trusted in God's protection and thought it would never happen to them. Before the day was over, the shop had burned to the ground. They had lost everything that they had invested in their business, built up so carefully over the years. Even all the stock was gone. Pamela was devastated and yet she was thankful that John's life had been spared. As the shock abated, Pamela realized more fully how God had protected her husband when he could so easily have been killed. Her friend called to tell her that her husband got up early that morning to pray for protection over John without knowing the reason why. Pamela was aware of God's hand on the situation. She felt very clearly that God had allowed this evil to go so far and no further when he spared John's life. Even in the midst of the trauma, she realized that he was there to take them through it. At the moment when a gun was held to his head, John did not know whether he would live or die. Despite his resistance to God, God had protected him. Pamela knew that the whole episode had shaken him deeply and brought him face to face with the call of God on his life. For that reason she hoped that some good might come out of the tragedy.

Yet her emotions were in turmoil. She began to feel that she could not trust anyone. No one could understand the emotional upheaval she was going through in the aftermath of the attack. The situation was made even worse because some business owners at the time had burned their own premises in order to claim insurance money. It took months to prove conclusively that Pamela and John were innocent and had nothing to do with it. Even some Christian friends became more distant during that time. Suspicion hurt. The only One Pamela could trust was God. Desperately she held onto him.

Gradually, the storm abated as the business reopened and they began to pick up their lives again. Something was missing, however. The sense of fulfillment in the business that had been there before never returned. Pamela's health took a turn for the worse and she decided to close the shop.

After the initial relief that John's life had been spared, the situation between the two of them deteriorated once more. Things got so bad that John gave her an ultimatum. She had to choose between him and God. Was this the end of the road?

At that time, a special week-long event was being held in a local church and unbelievably, John agreed to attend it with her. As she watched him during that week, Pamela could see similarities to her own situation all those years before when she had sat in meetings struggling with the whole issue of personal commitment to God. Pamela and John sat there together, like many other couples around them, listening to the clear challenge that was given, only to return home to bitter disagreements and rows about what they had heard.

On Sunday night John left the house, saying that he would never be back. He returned early on Monday morning and left for work as usual. Normally Pamela worked on Monday and was at home on Tuesday but that week her day off had been changed to Monday. She started phoning round friends and prayer groups, asking them to pray for John. Together they prayed and fasted that day.

On Tuesday, John was off work. It is a mark of John's personality that he does everything in a meticulous fashion and keeps his tools in immaculate working order. Because it was the month of May, one of the tasks for his day off was to mow the lawn. He had completed one round of the garden when the petrol lawnmower stalled. As he pulled the cord to start it up again, he heard his mother's voice saying clearly to him, "It is time to get right with God." By this stage both his parents had been dead for some years.

Pamela says, "I only wish you knew my husband because he is not the kind of person to imagine this kind of thing. He managed to get the mower going and did another round of the garden when it stalled again. This just does not happen to my husband's lawnmower—it is always in prime condition." This time he heard his father's voice repeating, "It is time to get right with God." He realized that God was speaking directly to him and that he could ignore it no longer. Leaving the lawnmower, he went into the kitchen, knelt down and handed over his life to the One who had refused to give up on him.

Usually when Pamela was leaving work she telephoned John to let him know what time she would be home. When she telephoned as usual on Tuesday afternoon, John warned her, "I have something to tell you when you get home."

Pamela's heart was full of dread as she entered the house, wondering what decision he had made. Perhaps he really had decided to leave for good. She sat down at the kitchen table and looked at him.

"What have you got to tell me?"

"Are you going to the prayer meeting tonight?"

"Yes, of course I'm going."

"Well, I'm going with you."

Pamela looked at him, disbelieving. As he related the story of the afternoon's events she began to cry. Suddenly realizing the full impact of what it meant, she leaped up, hugged him, laughed through her tears and thought, "Lord, you are able to do the impossible!"

Seventeen years of deep suffering gave way to unbelievable joy as she realized that God had at last answered all the prayers made on John's behalf. "God had given me that verse to keep me steady over the years, 'Be still, and know that I am God.' At last I really knew in a dramatic way that he was God. What a King we have!"

Things are very different in the Forrest home these days. John and Pamela have moved from the outward pretence that all is well, to the reality of sharing the most important aspect of their lives. It is such a change for Pamela to be able to share her faith with her husband, that sometimes she still stops and wonders at it. Instead of struggling and battling through life's difficulties on her own, they can now support each other as a couple as they bring their concerns to God in prayer together. Pamela finds it wonderful to look round in church, see John sitting there beside her and maybe catch his eye. It has been amazing for her to see how God has worked in her husband's life and how his attitude has changed. Pamela says, "Our home is completely different—there is so much love these days. It is honestly like a second honeymoon! I get excited when I think about God answering a certain prayer and say, 'John, can you see God doing that?' It is wonderful to have our faith in common. We come home from church and discuss the sermon together to explore what God is saying to us, not to fight about it. Sometimes these days when I am unwell and in pain John will put his hand on me and pray for me. It fascinates and excites me when he does that because it still touches me deeply to hear him pray—I haven't lost that wonder. It is amazing to be able to pray together for our children. As parents we all go through difficult times and it is wonderful for us to face them together now."

In recent years, Pamela has worked in a large, well-known department store. She is a buyer for ladies' fashion but is also in charge of the shoe department and the beauty hall. Moving there meant a much longer traveling time from home and at times she wondered if it was madness to take it on—but she felt strongly from the start that it was where God wanted her. She has found opportunities to share her faith with others in the store and has been greatly encouraged as she has seen situations turned round and God at work as Christians have prayed together. Through her work in this store, her own ministry has opened up in a variety of ways as people have come to know her story and invited her to share it with other women. She says, "It's wonderful but it frightens me too. It's a tremendous responsibility to stand in front of people and share what God has done."

With her interest in fashion and beauty, Pamela sometimes speaks to women's groups about the whole theme of outer and inner beauty. "While inner beauty is the most important, there is a role for outer beauty too. If someone is smartly dressed and well manicured, we notice. It is good for us to use our clothes and make-up to look the best we possibly can—as long as we put it in the right context."

Sometimes people will say to her in the shop, "You have a radiance. What make-up do you use?"

Her reply is usually the same: "My radiance is God. I am happy to tell you about my make-up but there is nothing like the beauty of God."

Pamela's beauty tips for women are based on creating something beautiful from very little. "That is how I see God," she says. "He can give us so much if we only ask him. I show the ladies how we can dress up a simple black dress with different accessories, handbags, scarves, belts, jewellery. We can start with very little but finish the look with something very striking and quite different using accessories. This is how God works in our lives. We may feel we have very little to offer, but when we hand it over to God he can turn it into something wonderful."

When Pamela shares some of the experiences through which God has led her, she finds she rarely speaks without someone from the audience coming up afterwards to tell her that they are going through a similar experience. "When I speak at meetings I say to people, 'Hold onto God. Keep on praying. Don't give up. God will never give us a trial that we are not able to bear. If you are going through a difficult time, think it a privilege and an honor to suffer for him, because your God knows that you are able to bear it.'"

She has noticed a change in recent years, with women being more open about their feelings, less afraid of showing their emotions. There is a hunger for the reality of God, not church or religion, but the reality of what God can do in a human life. Women want to be real before God and know God's presence real with them.

As parents and as husband and wife, John and Pamela face everything together now, knowing that God is in control and that he reigns in every area of their life. They have had to face painful times as their children have gone through difficulties in their own lives and, more recently, as Pamela's health has given them great concern.

Struggling with pain and weakness, Pamela could not help asking, "Why? Why this, after all we've been through?"

Just at the time when she was asking this question deep in her heart, a stranger who did not know her situation came up to her and said, "All things work together for good for those who love God." She and John have proved that to be true in the past and are trusting God together in this latest trial. Pamela does not want to miss what God is teaching her through her suffering. Is it in order that she can help others? Is it to teach her to wait on him more? She believes that whatever the final outcome, God is in control.

When she was in hospital recently, looking and feeling ghastly, she received wonderful texts from her daughter assuring her of her love and prayers for her return to health. Having that type of interaction with her daughter was a great encouragement to her.

"We need to leave our grown-up children in God's hands," she says. "We have to step back. And trust when it doesn't make sense."

Pamela feels now that as a young enthusiastic Christian she was very unwise. She was trying to live John's life for him. She wanted him to be the perfect Christian, to truly experience God, not just look the part. The more she tried to force him into that, the more he rebelled. Eventually she had to come to the stage of accepting that she could not do anything, God was the only One who could do it.

"I feel that if perhaps I had stepped back and not pressurized him I would not have pushed him into a corner where he felt he had to rebel. The more frustrated I got, the more difficult things became. John would show me his love in different ways and yet I was irritated—how could he show me love if he would not accept God's love? He became jealous of my love for God because it seemed to be taking me away from him."

When Pamela is talking to women these days she always says, "Step back and let God do it."

She also realizes now that in her initial enthusiasm as a new Christian she did not see how unwise it was to spend so much time at church. She admits that she should have been with her husband more, showing him the love of God instead of shutting him out of her life. That was not what God wanted her to do. It is a difficult balance to keep—as Christians we want to spend time with God and be with those who support us and offer us fellowship. Yet looking back with hindsight and maturity, Pamela can now understand why John reacted as he did. When women talk to her about this situation she hears the same thing over and over: "He won't do this, he won't go there, he won't come." She always says to them, "Don't push him." Then she adds, ruefully, "I was told that too and I didn't listen. I wish I had."

Pamela underlines the fact that we cannot change someone else's heart. We cannot force anyone into being a Christian. In fact, when we do try, it only drives them away—sometimes literally. No matter how hard Pamela tried to get John to go to a meeting, no matter how hard she tried to convince him that God was the answer to everything, it was all futile.

"The night before John became a Christian, as I was praying. I lifted my hands and physically lifted him up in my mind to God. I said, 'Here, God, take him. I can't do anything.' That physical lifting of hands was for me a symbolic handing over to God. Once I had done that, I felt immense relief. Already the burden lifted. I had come to the place where I was willing to wait on God. I was coming back to the verse of Scripture God had given me so long before, 'Be still, and know that I am God.' I was not just saying it but applying it. Having been a Christian for so many years of my life I know how easy it is to quote Scripture but it is only when we experience it from the heart and act on it that it becomes effective in our lives."

Having a husband who does not share your faith can at times be a painful and lonely experience. Pamela's advice is two-fold. On the one hand, hold onto your faith and continue to grow spiritually, making sure you have a strong support structure for yourself. On the other hand, be the wife and mother God wants you to be at home, showing his love by spending time with the family he has given you, sharing all their interests and concerns. Love and accept your husband as he is; consciously remind yourself of all his good points.

John and Pamela have been through some traumatic times in the family, times which have caused them great anguish of heart. The difference is that now they face such times together, united in the strength that comes from being one in Christ. To women with a husband who doesn't share their faith she says, "Be encouraged in God. He has a plan for each life. Never give up hope. God knows what he is doing. God is faithful. He will do what he has promised. He will answer prayer."

Be still, and know that I am God
Psalm 46:10

4.

I Believe in Miracles

Born to missionary parents who modeled the love of the God they served, Joanne found that the concept of relating to God as her heavenly Father came very naturally. As a child of seven, with her sister's help, she committed her young life to him. One Sunday someone from the Leprosy Mission spoke at her church, and as she realized the potential of a medical career, the desire was born in her heart to grow up to be a doctor and help those in need. Through her remaining years at school and in her early years at Queens University Belfast, that remained her primary focus.

When she left home and became a student, however, a very inspirational and creative time began for her as she discovered a new love of songwriting. She had been writing songs since she was fourteen, but now, with a wider experience of life, she began to write much more prolifically. Soon she began to face a dilemma—was medicine really what she wanted to do? It was a question she was to struggle with for the next five years. She could not bear to think of the disappointment it would be to her mother and father if she gave up medicine and yet her heart was drawn to the world of music. If God had given her the necessary talents to be a doctor, perhaps that was what he wanted her to do. Yet he had also gifted her musically. How was she to know which path to follow? Was it possible to do both?

In her third year at university, she decided to take a year out and work with Youth for Christ in Denmark. During that year she had many opportunities to sing, and became more and more convinced that music rather than medicine was her vocation. Towards the end of her time there, however, she developed nodules on her vocal chords and faced a choice of having laser surgery with the risk of possible damage to her voice, or resting her voice and giving up singing for a while. She took this to be God's guidance that she should return to her studies and finish her medical training while her voice recovered.

Joanne's return to Ireland was marked by her wedding to Stephen Hogg, one beautiful July day. Going back into medicine after her year out was something she did because she felt it was God's will rather than something that she really wanted to do. Options had been taken away because of the problem with her vocal chords.

Working as a junior doctor was a time of growing up as a person, as she came into close contact with the reality of life and death. She found she had greater responsibility and was more closely involved with patients in their hospital experience. It was a time of learning about people, about human nature, seeing how people deal with suffering, with and without God.

Six months into the job, she became ill. One day she collapsed at work and ended up as a patient in the cardiology ward where she had been a house officer. Faced with her symptoms, the doctor told her she had a viral condition that was affecting her heart, from which it could take anything from six months to two years to recover. For the next seven months, while she was off work, she prayed that God would show her what he wanted her to do with her life. For the first three months she was not well enough to go out unaided and for much of the time was confined to a third floor apartment on her own. She was confused by all that was happening to her, and in all the medical concerns her faith was tested and tried. She was learning to bring it all to God, and to experience the promised peace keeping her heart and mind as she trusted him.

Joanne went back to work in August and worked to the end of January to finish off her year as a house officer. At that stage she was still not fully fit medically so rather than go on to a job at the next level, she took some convalescence time with the intention of doing locums when she was feeling well enough. Over that period the door into music began to open up again. At the time Joanne, normally sporty and active, was frustrated by her physical limitations but looking back now, she can see God's hand in it all as the transition from medicine into music finally came about as a result of her illness.

During her year out in Denmark, the musician Adrian Snell had invited Joanne to be guest singer on an album he was recording and to perform at several of his concerts. That led to friendships with other musicians. Now, three years later, while Joanne was convalescing, two of these musicians contacted her. The island of Iona and the history of the early Christian church had inspired them musically but they felt that the duo was incomplete and remembered Joanne from three years before. The approach came at a significant time. Joanne was feeling increasingly that medicine was not her primary calling and was praying fervently that God would guide her clearly about the future. Within a few months she came to the place of leaving behind thoughts of medicine, aware of a strongly growing conviction that God was leading her forward into a new phase of life. Stephen, ever supportive, encouraged her in her decision to give up her well-paid job as a doctor to sing with an unknown Christian band. Iona's first album was released in the summer of 1990 and they went on to produce four albums over the next six years, with live performances in the United Kingdom, Europe and the United States.

One of their very early concerts was held in a wonderful big church in the south of England where the band was accommodated by members of the congregation, all in different houses. The arrangement was that on the morning after the concert the other members of the band would collect Joanne at ten o'clock in the morning from the house where she was staying. Ten o'clock came and went and there was no sign of them. Joanne was getting restless and frustrated that her plans were being held up when suddenly the phone rang and a lady asked to speak to her. It was a lady in her seventies who had been at the concert in the church the previous night.

"I'm glad I caught you," said the voice at the other end of the phone, "because during the concert while you were singing I felt God give me a word for you."

Immediately barriers went up in Joanne's mind. She had grown up in a conservative Christian family, with no experience of prophetic words, and regarded that whole area of Christian experience as rather questionable. Undeterred, the lady continued her story. "This is a strange message because it is very personal, so I spent much of the night praying about whether God really wanted me to speak to you."

"Well," conceded Joanne, "I suppose he must because I should not really still be here but the band is late coming to collect me."

"The word is 'The Lord will bless the fruit of your womb.' I don't think this is a word for now. I think it is something you will remember in the future."

Joanne thanked the lady and put down the phone. "Lord, confirm this in some way if it is from you," she prayed. The band arrived to collect her and she put it to the back of her mind. A couple of months later she met a friend who gave her a verse of Scripture from Isaiah 54 (v.1)

Sing, O barren woman,
   you who never bore a child;
burst into song, shout for joy,
   you who were never in labour.

She was brought up short as her mind connected the two messages. Having children was not an issue for her at that point, and as it did not seem immediately relevant, she decided that God would remind her of it in the future if it was significant. It did make her think, however. She was in her late twenties and had been married for five years. Was this God's time for them to start a family? It was confusing because she was just beginning something she believed God had called her to in the music scene. As she thought about the command "Sing ... burst into song ..." she saw the verse as confirmation that she was doing what God wanted her to do. For now, her singing was an acceptance of her barrenness. She carried on with her singing career, enjoying it, but with a little question at the back of her mind. She felt that others saw her as a career person, perhaps too caught up in her career to want to have a family, but ironically the reverse was really the case. She wanted a family but was content to concentrate on singing until it was God's time for her to have one.

For a number of years she carried on, not thinking too much about it. She and Stephen went on holiday to New Zealand and on their return, for the first time she thought she might be pregnant. Suddenly the possibility made her very excited. Almost afraid to discover that it was not true, she did not do a test immediately. She began imagining she had pregnancy symptoms. One month later her cycle resumed and she was back to normal, her body presumably having recovered from the effects of jet lag. The experience unleashed a flood of maternal desire that she had never known before. Until now she had been quite content with things as they were, but suddenly she was sure that it was God's time for them to start a family.

For almost a year, they tried for a baby, going through a roller-coaster of emotions every month. Joanne spent the first half of each month hoping she might conceive and the second half bitterly disappointed when it did not happen, but determined to try again the following month. So many people she knew seemed to be getting pregnant now and having babies. She was finding that increasingly difficult.

One day she discovered yet again that she was not pregnant. In the depths of despair, she went and sat outside in the yard. The dog came over and sat with his head in her lap, looking at her with big sad eyes. At that point, the postman came into the yard with an airmail letter from someone whose writing she did not recognize. It was a letter from a couple unknown to her who had followed Iona's progress over the years and had been praying particularly for Joanne. In this letter, the husband told Joanne about dreams he had had—in one, he saw her visibly pregnant singing on stage. In another, she was holding up a little baby boy who was obviously a very special gift to her. In yet another, she was sitting watching two children playing in her garden. The letter was spiritual and balanced, quoting a great deal of Scripture. As Joanne read it she felt that these were not fans with some strange ideas but rather that God had arranged it all as part of his amazing plan and attention to detail. Humanly speaking it was incredible that this letter would arrive on the day she was sitting with her head in her hands crying because she was not pregnant. She felt encouraged that even though things did not look promising just now, at some stage God had children in his plan for her.

A few months later Joanne again thought she might be pregnant but the test, as usual, was negative. Her emotions took the customary plunge. On that very day she received another letter from the same couple, this time written by the wife. The letter told about her prayers for Joanne and that God's word for her was "patience." She was not to give up hope because it would be a while before God's promise became reality. As Joanne read the letter she thought this might mean she would have to wait another six months. If she had known how long it would be, she would have found it harder to accept the word "patience." That letter, however, brought her closer to surrendering the whole thing to God and submitting to his plan. As she handed it over to him, she began to experience his peace. Her life at that point was filled with anxiety and stress because of the concern about childlessness—she had become obsessed with it. She saw babies and prams and pregnant women everywhere. She realized that she had allowed herself to become like that, stressed, anxious, emotional, taking her eyes off the Planner and trying to make her own plan.

"Family planning for some of us becomes a lesson that we cannot control everything in our lives," says Joanne. "Focusing on what we want to that extent and taking our eyes off God, we become a sitting duck for the enemy. 'Submit to God. Resist the devil and he will flee from you.' It's in that order. My submission and surrender of the situation to God was the first step I had to take in resisting the enemy. The attack came in not believing God loved me and had a plan for my life, in questioning his timing. That spiralled into guilt over not fulfilling my husband's desires and wondering if I was being punished. The enemy takes advantage of us like this when we take our eyes off God. Once I really desired to give myself to God's will I was able to resist that. Peace came and the enemy had to flee when I submitted my life to God."

That peace remained with Joanne over the next couple of years as she continued to sing. Her mother died during that time, shifting the focus from her preoccupation with becoming pregnant. It was actually other people's enquiries that eventually encouraged her to seek medical advice and begin some investigation into her infertility. In 1998, a year after her mother's death, she went to see a consultant, who checked her hormone levels and confirmed that she had probably not been ovulating since her mother died.

At first, Joanne resisted her suggestion of a laparoscopy, deciding instead to try hormone therapy for six months. By June 1999 this was obviously having no effect so she agreed to undergo a laparoscopy. During this procedure the doctors tried without success to get dye through her fallopian tubes. Afterwards they told her that it would be virtually impossible for her ever to have children naturally. Joanne was devastated. How could that be when God had given her all those reassuring messages? Had she misunderstood what he was saying?

The diagnosis was reinforced by other investigations. That summer she ended up having the laparoscopy in June, a hysteroscopy in August—which showed her womb was normal inside and gave a glimmer of hope—and then a hysterosalpingogram a month later. Her father drove her to the hospital and sat in the car while this third procedure was carried out. As she lay on the table she was able to watch the screen and see dye flowing inside her, her womb filling up and then tubes like two coils of spaghetti with no dye coming out through the other end. The earlier findings of the laparoscopy were confirmed beyond doubt. The visual impact of this dye test was much more profound on Joanne because she could see for herself what they were dealing with. She knew what normal fallopian tubes should look like and these were completely abnormal. She says, "God let me see the concrete medical evidence that it was impossible for me to have a child." She went out to the car and told her father the results. Gently he took her hand and prayed with her about it there in the hospital car park.

The worst point for Joanne had been immediately after receiving the results of the laparoscopy because it was the first time she had to deal with the physical impossibility of having children. The hysteroscopy had given a little temporary shred of hope but the third test was the final confirmation that she would never, naturally speaking, have children of her own. It was at this point that Joanne really took hold of the word that had been given to her ten years earlier, "The Lord will bless the fruit of your womb." She still had some doubts about it. "When you have the evidence staring you in the face you begin to wonder if the message was about spiritual fruit rather than physical. And yet this word 'womb' was a very particular anatomical physical detail. I had to believe that God was talking about physical children." Humanly, she went through a period of grieving and yet alongside the human sorrow was the belief deep in her heart that God could do anything. Believing in God's omnipotence in her head did not completely alleviate the pain of facing the reality of a body that did not work normally.

It looked as though, apart from miraculous intervention, IVF was the only other possibility. Joanne believed God had promised her long ago that there would be blessing for her children. Now, some ten years later, her faith was challenged as she and Stephen wrestled with the decision. Did they hold onto this promise regardless of the condition of her body or were they meant to go down the road of medical intervention? God's Word to her did not specify how she would have children. By this stage, she was thirty-six years old and conscious that time was running out. After much thought and prayer they decided to go ahead and embark on IVF.

As Christians, they had some ethical questions about it. After praying about it, however, they made the decision that whatever embryos were created as a result of the treatment, they would be committed to having them put back into

Joanne's body. They prayed that God would only allow the creation of embryos that they could use. It was a traumatic procedure for both of them.

Wheels were set in motion pretty quickly for IVF because of Joanne's age and because medically it was the only option. The whole procedure was costly financially and at one stage the doctors suggested they should not complete the particular treatment because Joanne was not responding to the drugs. Joanne, however, was determined to give it the best shot they could. They managed to get two eggs and then had to wait for thirty-six hours to see if they had been fertilized. When the phone call came through that one had been fertilized and they had one embryo, Joanne and Stephen were overjoyed. They could see God's hand in it all—this was surely the child God had for them. When the embryo was put into her body, Joanne immediately felt that they had a child; this embryo had all the potential of a human being. Once that had happened, she knew she was pregnant. Of course she received the embryo just after fertilization so most people would not even know they were pregnant at that stage. There   followed a very long two weeks waiting to see if the embryo would implant successfully in her womb. If it did not, she would have withdrawal bleeding, showing that the process had been unsuccessful.

Just after the embryo was put back in her womb, during those two weeks while she was waiting to see if the embryo would survive, Joanne had a very special experience of God. Walking up the lane near her home one February morning, around the time of the anniversary of her mother's death, she stopped to pick snowdrops from the side of the road. She had been having a quiet time of prayer and meditation as she walked. All of a sudden she stopped in her tracks because out of nowhere she clearly heard a voice speaking the name "Isaac." It seemed like a physical voice. She actually said,

"God, was that you?" It was so clear that she felt there was no other explanation. Her response was, "OK, Lord, if we have a son then that is what he will be called." She held this in her heart, not sharing it with anyone, not even her husband at this stage, but the experience increased her expectation that this embryo was Isaac, the promised son.

The days passed one at a time, and four days beyond the expected time there was still no bleeding. Joanne was now happily sure she was finally pregnant. At five o'clock one morning she was awake, excitedly visualizing life with this long-awaited child, when she realized that she had not yet done a pregnancy test to confirm everything. Quickly she climbed out of bed and did the test. Unbelievably, it was negative. Surely not. Stunned, she climbed back into bed and sobbed her heart out. Stephen tried desperately to comfort her—maybe it was too early to show up on the test. After all, she had had no bleeding. Hoping against hope, she rang the hospital.

"No, Joanne, you are not pregnant," was the response. "Sometimes this happens, the bleeding does not occur for a few days." Actually it was a full week before it happened, every day adding to the emotional trauma of it all. Because Joanne had felt that she really had a baby at that point, and was emotionally incubating the baby, she mourned the loss of this little life, gone almost before it had begun. The miracle for Joanne and Stephen was that this was the first time ever that their genetic make-up had actually been combined. Was it a boy or a girl? Which of them would he or she have looked like? They would never know the answer to those questions. It was the closest they had ever come to having a baby.

So much hope had been generated during the whole process that Joanne had really begun to believe that this was God's way of fulfilling his promise. When they eventually found that there was no pregnancy, however, it was devastating. All their hopes were dashed once more, this time seemingly irrevocably. As Joanne prayed and cried about it her one thought was, "I can't go through this again." Quietly she felt God saying to her, "You don't have to." When her hormone levels were checked a few months later, they were even less favorable for a successful outcome so further treatment was out of the question. Still Joanne struggled with the question: "Many Christian couples have successful IVF treatment. Why not me?" The answer seemed to be, "This is not my way for you." Gradually she accepted that this was the voice of the Holy Spirit speaking to her. Acceptance of that voice allowed God's peace back in to restore her faith.

She picked up her life and was on tour with the band when God intervened again. Four months after the failure of IVF, Iona was doing a concert at Greenbelt festival in England. While she was singing, Joanne suddenly had an incredible sense of the presence of God and a joy in her spirit that had her almost laughing while she sang.

After the concert, one of the band members found her and told her that a lady in the audience that evening had been drawn to the sound of the music and had sensed God's presence in a special way. She said to one of the band, "I'm not the kind of person that these things happen to, but I feel I have to give a message to someone. Tell Joanne to remember Abraham and Sarah. I have no idea if this is of any significance to Joanne but she will know if it is."

Joanne says, "As soon as I heard the message I felt my heart leaping inside me. I immediately thought of God's promise to Abraham and Sarah that they would have a son called Isaac. I thought of my own promise of Isaac. I had not told anybody about the name Isaac at this stage; I had just written about it in my journal. I would have told Stephen at some stage during the pregnancy but hadn't yet. This word from a stranger who knew nothing about me or my history was so personal that it was something only God could have known about. To get this word from her was really mind blowing. To me it was a deeply personal confirmation that the whole matter was in God's hands."

During this time, some people were encouraging Joanne to seek prayer for healing. Surely if she believed God could heal her she should seek out someone with a gift of prayer and healing and ask them to pray specifically for her? Joanne was reluctant to do this. "It was just too personal a matter. I felt that if God wanted someone to pray for me he would bring the person to me—someone who didn't know my story." She was looking for confirmation that God wanted to do a miracle for her.

A month after the incident at the festival, she traveled to Guatemala on a mission trip with a group doing medical and evangelistic work. She went with an anticipation that God would do something special for her during this time. She kept a fairly low profile for the two weeks she was there but in Guatemala God spoke to her about the centrality of the person of Jesus in her life. She realized that in the course of the previous years of disappointment and grief, she had depersonalized her faith. She had held onto the Creator God in control of everything but had moved away from an intimate relationship with Christ as Lord.

At the end of those two weeks the desire to be really close to Jesus again became her greatest longing, to the extent that she wanted that more than she wanted a baby. "I felt that I was eventually getting my priorities sorted out. Having a close living relationship with Jesus was more important to me than any other single thing."

At the end of the trip, Pat, one of the missionaries, asked Joanne if she could pray with her before she left. During that prayer, she laid her hands on Joanne and asked that God would bless Joanne and Stephen's marriage with a child. As she prayed Joanne felt a very powerful sensation, almost like a physical burning, go through her body. She believes that at that point God did something miraculous.

"I will be waiting to hear your good news," were Pat's parting words.

"You know I've been told that it is impossible physically?"

"I don't have a problem with that. Do you?"

"No, I don't," Joanne replied.

On her return, Joanne felt that she had to share with others what she believed God had done. Her faith was strong and her expectations high because of all that had happened and sharing her excitement at what God was going to do was a natural response. Not all responded as she hoped, however. People tended to be skeptical, including Stephen who was very afraid that her hopes would be dashed again. In October she felt unwell and began to wonder if she was pregnant. When that proved not to be the case, she was very disappointed. That same day she received an email from Pat, with whom she had had no communication since her trip to Guatemala in August. In this wonderful letter, Pat described how she had felt a special burden to pray for Joanne on the previous day. She had prayed for the fulfillment of God's promise and in her letter quoted the Bible passage about Hannah dedicating the child Samuel to God. She had named him Samuel because he was God's gift to her. The reference to Samuel was astounding to Joanne. She had already decided that as well as the name Isaac, her son should be called John Samuel after his two grandfathers. The disappointment this time was fleeting because she was convinced that it was still going to happen. This letter arriving just when she needed it was another confirmation that God was in control. Leaving the whole matter with him, she threw herself into other things, planning another trip to New Zealand and more concerts with Iona in the fall.

In November, before they went on vacation, an older lady whom Joanne knew slightly contacted her by phone. She said, "I've been wanting to contact you for a year now but I was waiting for God to prompt me when the time was right."

They talked about music ministry in general and how God's anointing seemed to be on certain musicians in a special way. Then the lady went on, "The time is coming now in God's plan for the seed that you will bear."

"Do you know my history?" Joanne was taken aback.

"No, that is just the message I have for you." The lady then proceeded to talk about "the Isaac ministry."

"God gave me that name in February," said Joanne. "I believe that will be my son's name." The lady became very excited at the other end of the telephone. She encouraged Joanne to pray for God's anointing and to anoint Stephen and herself with oil. Joanne says, "God was challenging me about many things that were not part of my experience but by then I was open to just about anything because I had received so many words from him. Some of the ways God uses are strange—Jesus spat in the dust and put it on eyes and there are many references to anointing with oil in Scripture. I decided to act on my friend's advice. In the room where we were staying on holiday there was even a little bottle of massage oil. I came home from New Zealand with a very strong sense that something had happened when we were there."

Soon after she arrived back from New Zealand, Joanne began feeling strange and sick, unlike anything she had ever felt before. She had already decided not to do any more pregnancy tests until she knew for certain that she was pregnant because she had had so many disappointments. This time she was certain. At the same time, seeing a positive test with her own eyes was hard to take in after seeing so many negative ones in the past. It was almost a year exactly since God had given her the name Isaac. She ran up the lane by their house into the field, overcome with a wonderful sense of exhilaration. Unable to wait to tell Stephen at the end of the day and wanting to see his face at the news, she persuaded him to come home from work at lunch time. Disbelieving, he persuaded her to do another test before he would accept that it was actually true.

Joanne was sure the baby was going to be a boy and there was no debate about names! Isaac John Samuel was born in September 2001. It was only later that Joanne realized all three biblical characters had been born to women who had been described as barren. The following year she was pregnant again and Ethan was born in May 2003.

"I suppose that means you're fixed now," commented Stephen.

All the challenges to her faith in the days before she became a mother do not seem so great now compared to the challenges Joanne faces each day.

"If I needed God before I certainly need him more now! In some ways motherhood seems to have brought out the worst in me and shown me what a long way I have to go to become more like Christ in my everyday living. I had become self-centred and impatient—I thought after all those lessons God had finished with me in that area. Learning patience and relying on him for wisdom and understanding is even more essential in my life now."

While she feels the boys are God-given in a special way, Joanne acknowledges that they are normal children who test her patience and wisdom on a daily basis. At those times she thinks back to "the Isaac ministry" and when she wonders if they will ever survive all the childhood accidents she thinks of the promise, "The Lord will bless the fruit of your womb." The promise was not just for before the children were born but remains increasingly relevant as they grow up. God's promises to her remain with her continually.

Joanne decided to take a break from Iona after Isaac was born, apart from occasional concerts. She says, "I was forty, I'd had two children in two years, and that was all I had energy for!" In 2004 she did some European concerts but on principle she was not willing to leave the boys to go on tour. By 2006, however, the boys were a little more independent and a new Iona CD came out in October of that year. Iona still does a few concerts each year but it has much less momentum as the children are Joanne's main focus. Musically God has been leading her in a different direction as she uses her gifts in praise and worship. She is also working on a solo project which is more compatible with having a family and hopes to have her second solo CD out by the end of 2007.

Like all mothers, she struggles to balance her responsibilities to family and home with the use of her God-given gifts outside the home. She says, "The children are an absolute delight. They are happy, contented little boys. It is wonderful to see God's blessing in their lives. Personally I am concentrating on pursuing God and knowing him more deeply. I have a real hunger for him. I am trusting him to lead me into a more spiritual life, studying Scripture and spending time with him rather than being the busy action person I have been in the past. That's where I am now."

Joanne's story is irrefutable evidence that just occasionally, God chooses to intervene in human life in ways that we cannot understand or explain. It reminds us that the God who created us is still the God of miracles and we can trust him to work out his purposes in our lives and families.

Many years ago, J.B. Phillips wrote a book entitled *Your God is Too Small*[3] in which he suggested that we have substituted our limited vision of God for the all-powerful creator God of the universe. Joanne's story encourages us to a larger view of the God we serve and trust. She says, "We never surprise God but it is great when he surprises us!"

"For I know the plans I have for you," declares the LORD,
"plans to prosper you and not to harm you,
plans to give you hope and a future."
Jeremiah 29:11

5.

Black Dog

As Suzanne cuddled her baby son close to her and looked into his face in amazement, the whole world seemed wonderful. She and Rick had been married for three and a half years before Nathan was born and his arrival had brought them supreme happiness. Of course, for the first few months he disturbed their sleep and often interrupted their plans with his needs, but it was the joy Suzanne felt when she held him in her arms that amazed her. It was beyond anything she had ever imagined.

Eighteen months before Nathan was born, Suzanne had ceased working as a solicitor in order to pursue her PhD. Now that he was nine months old she was taking up her research again but she was finding it more difficult than she had anticipated to resume her studies. She tried to work from home so that she did not have to leave Nathan more than necessary and her father was very helpful, looking after him for a couple of afternoons each week when his flexible working hours permitted it. When her father was not there, she worked when Nathan was sleeping in the afternoon or evening but found it difficult to distance herself mentally from house and baby in order to study.

A month after she started studying again she became unwell with an inner ear infection, causing nausea and dizziness. Rather than passing quickly, as Suzanne expected, it dragged on for several months. If she tried to sit at the computer or read for more than half an hour at a time she became ill. Her studies were seriously disrupted, leaving her very frustrated. In October, just as she thought she was finally recovering, she realized that she was expecting a second baby. Deciding that trying to study with a second one on the way was going to cause her too much pressure, she reluctantly put the idea of a doctorate to one side and decided to be a full-time mother.

The second pregnancy was very different to the first. At about seven weeks she had a scare when she almost lost the baby. An early internal scan showed that there was still a heartbeat but there was no way to tell if the baby was going to survive or not. This uncertainty continued intermittently for the first three months. The weeks leading up to Christmas were a protracted time of tension, as she watched every day, wondering whether the baby was going to live or not. At twelve weeks, the scan was reassuring and from January to Easter all seemed well.

At the end of April, Nathan moved from the nursery into his own bedroom, a natural progression to another stage of his life. Suzanne did not sleep well that night and felt sick and tired the next day. As this pattern was repeated for the next few nights, she began to worry about not sleeping. How was she going to look after Nathan the next day if she could not sleep at night? He was an active two-year-old; he tired her out during the day, even when she was fully rested. Her mother, father, and husband were all working so she knew she had to get up the next morning and look after him no matter how she felt. Worrying about it made the situation worse. Some nights she would sleep for about an hour altogether and get up the next morning feeling shattered. The final two months of her pregnancy were marked by a daily cycle of anxiety, sleeplessness, exhaustion, and depression. Suzanne knew that many people, feeling awkward and uncomfortable, do not sleep well towards the end of pregnancy but this was different. She spent the nights lying staring into space until she could bear it no more and got up to watch television. Sitting on her own there through the night hours or wandering anxiously round the house, she became fearful and troubled.

As her distress increased, the doctor prescribed sleeping tablets but told her to try not to take them every night. She was reluctant to take them anyway because of the pregnancy although the doctor assured her that the ones he prescribed would not do the baby any harm. She oscillated between sleeping with the help of medication, and sleeplessness without it. Some nights she did not sleep even when she took it. Towards the end of the pregnancy, she stopped taking it completely and persuaded herself to lie down and rest even if she could not sleep. She would sleep for a short time, wake, get up to change her position, go back to bed, have another short sleep, then get up again. Each morning she got out of bed to drag herself through another day. The last two months seemed to last for ever. She tried everything that was recommended. She had a bath before going to bed every night. She sprinkled lavender profusely around the bedroom. She got out of bed and walked around when she felt restless. Desperate for the pregnancy to end, she was greatly relieved when Daniel decided to come a week before his due date. He was born on June 30 2006.

It was a straightforward delivery. Suzanne went into hospital at 8.30 in the morning and Daniel was born at 11.50. Everything went very smoothly, with little pain relief apart from gas and air. As she went for a bath afterwards Suzanne felt relief that it was all over so quickly and that all was well but exhaustion seemed to have affected her feelings. She was happy that Daniel was born, but in a detached way. She felt numb, dazed and not quite sure why she felt so removed from everything.

She got little rest that day. She was surrounded by visitors during the afternoon and evening. As she watched everyone else holding Daniel and looking so happy she felt as if she was out of the loop. She smiled at everyone as expected but could feel nothing. She put it down to tiredness, the accumulation of weeks of sleeplessness. There was little sleep that night either, however, as the noise in her twelve-bed ward seemed to continue all night. Next morning, Suzanne decided that she had had enough, gathered up her new son, and twenty-four hours after giving birth was at home again.

It was a shock to the system to be back in the normal run of things so quickly. When she opened the fridge, the milk from the day before was still there and useable. What had happened here? It seemed unreal that she had had a baby and was back in the kitchen again. The next day, Sunday, she threw herself into being busy. In between breastfeeding Daniel she rushed around preparing tea and biscuits for the dozen visitors that turned up, while maintaining a flow of conversation.

"How was the delivery?"

"Fine, great, no problems."

That was true as far as pain was concerned, she thought. She did not feel fine in other ways but she did not have time to think about it. This was what you did when you had your second child, you just got on with it.

Rick went out to church that Sunday night. All of a sudden, as Suzanne sat there at home on her own she began to worry—what if it was not the pregnancy that had been keeping her awake? What if she had somehow lost the ability to sleep and would not sleep properly ever again? Waves of panic began to roll over her as she felt as if something catastrophic was about to happen.

She lay awake all that night, and of course, was exhausted the next day. Desperately she phoned a friend who was part of her church home group. Over the last few months of the pregnancy she had prayed for and with Suzanne and had been a great source of help and support.

"How are you?" Gail was concerned.

"Not great," admitted Suzanne.

That evening, Gail and one of the church elders came to see her and together they prayed for God to touch her body and mind and give her sleep. That night she slept better than she had for a long time and from that day on had very little problem sleeping. But for some reason the feeling of anxiety remained.

During both pregnancies, Suzanne felt unwell and lost her appetite. Conscious of the baby, she tried to eat reasonably well but did not enjoy anything except fruit. She envied other people who had a good appetite while they were pregnant. After Nathan was born she recovered her appetite immediately and ate everything in sight, from the horrible hospital food to chocolates and food that visitors brought her. When Daniel was born, however, her appetite did not return. She poked at her food without enjoyment. She tried to make herself eat because she was feeding Daniel, but it was a struggle. She could not understand why she was reacting in such a strange way—she felt totally different to the way she had after her first baby. For the first few days, she felt rather stunned and did not know what to make of it all. She was still adjusting to the idea of the baby actually being here. On the Monday after Daniel was born, she felt low all day and could not gather herself together to do anything. When the community midwife came on Tuesday, she tried to explain: "I don't feel normal. It's not the same as it was with Nathan." After Nathan she had experienced the "third day blues" like most mothers but then recovered her equilibrium without any problem. Not this time. She appreciated the opportunity to sit and talk to the midwife who advised her to see her own doctor. He knew her history, as she had seen him several times during the pregnancy.

Hoping that he could help, Suzanne made an appointment to see him a few days later. As he listened to her story he told her that she might be suffering from depression, which although not much talked about, can actually start before the baby is born. Looking back, Suzanne felt that this was indeed the case; she had been feeling so miserable and yet no one had suggested that there might be a problem before the baby was born. There seemed to be a general reluctance to talk about signs of antenatal depression.

At first she was unwilling to accept the doctor's diagnosis or to agree to take antidepressants. She was shocked at the whole idea of the word "depression." Understanding that she needed time to process the idea, the doctor just nodded and said, "If you are feeling no better in a week come back and see me. Maybe it is just tiredness after the birth and getting back into everything so quickly."

Suzanne left the surgery, met Rick for coffee and sat and cried in the coffee shop as she told him what the doctor had said. She could not bear the stigma of having depression.

"This will be with me for the rest of my life," she wept. "It will be down in my records and everyone will know. It will define me for ever more."

She was embarrassed and ashamed at the very suggestion. Grimly she told herself that it must be something else; she could get over it. She struggled through the next four or five days before admitting that she needed the doctor's proffered help. About a week after her first visit, she phoned him back. "I can't cope, I do need something to help me." As she reluctantly accepted the prescribed antidepressants, he warned her that it could be some time before she would feel completely well again. This was underlined by the community midwives who were a great support in the early days. Although a different one came to see her most days, they updated each other on her condition and some stayed for a long time talking and listening. Through all this, Suzanne's doctor was very patient and helpful, seeing her regularly to discuss how she was feeling.

Concerned about the possible effect of the antidepressants on Daniel, Suzanne consulted the internet which did nothing to alleviate her fears. According to some websites, the advice was to stop breastfeeding when on medication. Desperately wanting to continue feeding Daniel herself, she welcomed her own doctor's advice to carry on if that was what she wanted to do and if it helped her feel better. She is glad now that her doctor took that approach because for much of those early months, feeding Daniel was the only thing she felt she could do well. It gave her some feeling of fulfillment rather than coping with guilt about having to give that up too. She says, "In the past, babies were probably put onto a bottle automatically if the mother was on medication but I can see that it could be very difficult for the mother—something else for her to beat herself up about. On top of feeling you can't cope with life, you cannot even manage to feed your own child. That would have been very hurtful to me." At the same time, Suzanne acknowledges that everyone is different and what worked for her may not necessarily be best for someone else. In individual cases such decisions should be made together by parents with medical advice in the best interests of both mother and child at this stage.

She continued to suffer from a constant feeling of anxiety which hung over her like a black cloud. This peaked into regular waves of more extreme fear, removing all sense of enjoyment from her normal life. When Daniel was six days old, Suzanne and Rick went into town with him for the first time, to the delight of many who stopped to admire the new baby and ask about his age and weight. All Suzanne knew was that she felt panicky; she did not want anyone to ask her anything about him; she did not want to talk to them. With Nathan she had been so proud when she took him out, she had loved to talk about him, but now she felt she had to put on a fake smile and make an attempt at conversation— yes, it was great, it was busy with the two children but they were all delighted, everything was wonderful. She was covering up, managing to talk but inside felt as if she was in pieces. Something strange was going on. Something was badly wrong.

Before Daniel was born, Suzanne remembered being out in the car with Rick and Nathan, looking forward to the next baby and talking excitedly with Rick about how great it would be to be a little family of four. Now Daniel was in the baby car seat in front beside Rick, and Suzanne sat in the back with Nathan. On car journeys during the first few weeks after Daniel was born, Suzanne would look round at them all, thinking how great this should be. Desperately she searched for some kind of awareness of the happiness she knew she should feel. Logically, she tried to force herself to feel happy. Here she was with two healthy children and a great husband. Everything was fine. Yet no matter how much she enumerated all her blessings she could never quite get there. What on earth was wrong with her? On the surface everything was fine but she felt so far from fine she could not convince herself that things were right. During the first few weeks she spent much of the time going over and over all the things that were good in her life and trying to analyze what was wrong. She felt guilty at her inexplicable feelings of despair when she had so much for which to be thankful.

She could not shake off the feeling that something dreadful had happened or was about to happen. What was it? She could not pinpoint anything in particular; she was now sleeping reasonably well, yet she felt everything was wrong. Sometimes it even felt as if there was no point to

life. Every morning as she woke it would hit her in a rush—
it had been so difficult to get through the previous day and
now she would have to make the effort all over again for the
coming day. Sometimes she thought she could not face
another day like that, struggling through, feeling terrible
and going to bed again. Was it worth it? She felt worthless
and hopeless.

That summer the days that were inevitably worse were those
that should have been special, when they were out for the day,
doing something together as a family. Those were the days
when she would spend the time trying to convince herself that
she was having a good time but wondering in frustration why
she was not enjoying herself. The mundane days for which she
did not have any high expectations blended into each other in a
grey blankness but at least she avoided the disappointment that
accompanied a day that should have been different. Long car
journeys were the worst because she had too much time to
think. She was constantly saying to Rick, "Talk to me, talk to me
about something" because she knew that her whole mood
would go down if she just sat thinking. Without something def-
inite to occupy her mind, she would immediately start to worry.
She had to keep it focused on something else. Poor Rick was
under pressure to maintain a constant stream of conversation in
order to keep her in a reasonable frame of mind.

One day in the middle of July, they had a family outing to
the seaside. In the afternoon they wandered round a furniture
shop, looking for a couple of pieces of furniture for the
lounge. Normally Suzanne loved looking at things for the
house and often she and Rick would go out and spend an
afternoon looking at what was available. That day, however,
she felt completely empty. She tried to conjure up any feeling
of interest in what she was looking at but somehow she felt
totally blank, as if there was no point in what they were

doing. The feeling terrified her. It was as if there was nothing inside. There was no part of her that was enjoying anything or looking forward to anything. She had an overwhelming feeling of a dark weight pushing her down. As she walked around the shop that day she was thinking desperately, "Somebody please help me." She wished someone somewhere would notice that something was wrong and ask her if she was all right. It was as if she was walking around in a black cloud. She felt so detached from her surroundings that she wanted to reach out and touch somebody going past to make life feel real. It was a very frightening experience. She struggled to explain her feelings to Rick, finding it very difficult to put into words—still not quite understanding what was happening to her or how to articulate it. Defeated, she retreated inside herself and fought overwhelming waves of panic as they headed home in the car.

One of the symptoms that many mothers experience with postnatal depression is difficulty in bonding with their baby. Suzanne, however, went to the other extreme and refused to be separated from him. While he was a small baby, she carried him round the shops for two or three hours at a time. He spent his life on her shoulder because she did not want to put him down. Because she was breastfeeding him, he slept beside her in bed every night so that when he woke she did not have to get up to feed him. She hated being up in the middle of the night by herself. He slept really well beside her and Suzanne drew great comfort from having him so close. She was reluctant to tell midwives about this sleeping arrangement, however, knowing that it was not generally acceptable and that he should really be put back in his cot after he was fed. Having him beside her was part of her coping mechanism. She felt that it was the only way she could get through the night. In some strange way he was her security. Almost by holding him she could convince herself that because he was real, everything was fine; he was healthy and she loved him. He was hardly out of her sight for the first few months of his life. She thought, "This can't be postnatal depression because I have such a strong bond with him." That thought brought a new concern. If she was not experiencing some of the classic symptoms of postnatal depression, did that mean she was imagining the whole thing? Was this just how she was going to feel from now on? The only thing more frightening than having postnatal depression was not having it and discovering that this terrible anxiety that gripped her was going to be a permanent part of her life. The other worry was what would happen when Daniel began to sleep through the night. "How am I going to get through the night without him? How will I cope when he has to go into his own room?"

Through most of her waking hours, Suzanne worried about everything in the future, especially anything that stood out as a major event. She refused to plan ahead. She did not want to think about the next day or even listen to anyone talk about what they might be doing the next day, because she knew she would worry about it. Anything in the future caused her anxiety, particularly the fear that she might not sleep thinking about it. For that reason, for example, she refused to invite people to the house ahead of time. She could cope if she invited them spontaneously but she would not make an arrangement for even a short time ahead. She was afraid that it would become a big thing in her head and put her off her sleep. She had never felt like this before but suddenly the whole area of planning became a major issue.

For two or three months she did not do her usual weekly grocery shopping because it entailed planning ahead for meals. Instead she bought food on the day she needed it. It seemed ridiculous to others because it was impossible for people looking on from the outside to understand. Why could she not just get over it and go out and do her weekly shop like everyone else?

The only explanation Suzanne could give, even to herself, was that it was another coping mechanism. When she felt so mixed up in herself, she had to do what made her feel even a tiny bit more comfortable. If that meant shopping on a daily basis instead of weekly, then it was worth it.

She hated being on her own and constantly wanted people around her. The situation was all slightly less intense when she was at someone else's house so she ended up not wanting to be in her own house at all. Something about the company and normality of other people's lives was comforting. Even though as a teacher Rick was at home all summer, she also wanted her parents around and spent most of that summer with them, hating to leave their house because returning home meant coming back to the dreaded evening and night time. Although she was now sleeping better, memories of the fearsome nights during her pregnancy still haunted her. The fear of being alone increased as the end of summer approached, and with it the end of the long teachers' holidays. How would she cope on her own with the children when Rick went back to school? She was not concerned that she would not be able to look after the children but she worried about the effect on herself—she would have no one around to distract her from thinking. She had spent the whole summer trying not to think. Only by being with other people and talking all the time could she manage to avoid anxiety-inducing thoughts.

The night before Rick returned to school she was wakeful and anxious, fearful that if she had a sleepless night she would go back to how she felt at the beginning. Once he was back at school, however, and they were into a routine she realized that she could actually manage on her own and the world did not fall in around her. She tried to keep her routine as constant as possible, with a terror of anything that threatened the way things were at the moment, fearing that the slightest change would set her back. If she could keep each day reasonably the same then she could hold on. Anything out of the ordinary shook her. Even normally pleasant experiences were a problem—her niece's birthday, her cousin's wedding, any big occasion became a possible threat that might make things worse.

Her doctor continued to be a source of strength and encouragement. One day he said, "There will come a point where you will forget to worry for a few minutes. Suddenly you will realize you've stopped worrying for a moment and then those moments will get longer and happen more often." Very gradually Suzanne began to realize that the doctor's words were coming true. Often she was frustrated by the slowness of her recovery, wondering wearily why she was still not better. Although the doctor had warned her it might be a while before she began to feel better, she worried that the antidepressants were not working—not only were things bad but now even the antidepressants were not helping. That gave her something else to worry about. Sometimes she was annoyed that the doctor had not spelt out for her more clearly at the beginning how long the recovery would take. On reflection, however, she realized that perhaps she could not have coped with such a prognosis at the outset. It was hard to accept even at this stage. "Please let there be a change instantly," she would pray. "I cannot wait for weeks."

At the end of September, the doctor increased the dose of her medication slightly, causing her a new worry about its possible long-term effects.

"How do I keep going, taking all this medicine and not feeling any better?" she began to wonder. For a couple of bad days she had a fear that she would fall completely out of reach so that no one could help her. She was in despair. As the weeks passed, however, she began to feel more like herself as the increased medication began to take effect. She began to enjoy parts of the day although she was still conscious of a vague cloud always on the horizon and some days were more difficult than others. Sometimes she had three or four bad days in a row but then for a couple of days she felt that things were improving. The slightest little thing could affect her either way so that within any one day, her moods could go from feeling reasonably happy to being down in the depths.

It was November before she began to put any photographs of Daniel into an album. It was the first time that she had really looked back at his early baby photographs. She worked with them quickly and then went and did something else because she found it so difficult to look at the pictures of him as a small baby. She found it distressing to think, "Why did it have to be like that? Why could I not have enjoyed it? Those should have been wonderful moments during the first few weeks—I've lost those and I can't get them back." He was a great baby, easy to manage, happy and content in contrast to his mother's despair.

Before Daniel was born, Suzanne's friend Jane had been a great support, helping to look after Nathan during that time when she was unable to sleep and feeling exhausted. She was disappointed to be on holiday when Daniel was born and on her return called to see Suzanne and the new baby. Taking Daniel on her lap she looked appraisingly at Suzanne.

"He is lovely. How are you?"

"I feel dreadful."

"I'm not surprised. You were so low and tired towards the end of your pregnancy I couldn't see how you were going to bounce back again immediately."

Cuddling Daniel, Jane went on to share that after her own second baby was born she was diagnosed with postnatal depression and was on antidepressants for months. Suzanne was amazed. This competent and capable mother who coped so well and juggled so many things in her life had been depressed? The evidence of complete recovery from postnatal depression was staring her in the face. If Jane could recover so well, then perhaps she could too. That broke the stigma for Suzanne. She thought, "Maybe everyone who has this is not completely nuts." She admitted to herself that that had been her fundamental fear. Perhaps because of the general reluctance to admit to it, perhaps because of extreme cases seen in the soaps where a child is taken into care in case the mother harms it, she had regarded postnatal depression with revulsion, an illness that marked her out as abnormal. Talking to Jane that day, Suzanne realized that it happens to many people who are quite normal. Psychologically it was a breakthrough. For the first time she was able to think, "Others get over it. I'll be fine." It was not that easy but it was the first glimmer of hope that some day things would be better.

Since that time, a number of other people have said to Suzanne, "Me too. I was like that years ago." Suzanne says: "Sometimes I wish that I had known all this before it happened; it would have saved me so much heartache. It is much more common than anybody realizes. So many people are afraid to mention it that often only close family know. People don't want others to think there is something wrong with them. They say, 'We'll deal with it ourselves.' That is one of the worst ways of coping because you need people to know so that others who have been there can share how they got through it. Smiling and pushing it down, trying to block it, is not helpful."

While Jane's story came as a great relief at the time and helped Suzanne deal with the fact that she had postnatal depression, that in itself did not alleviate the symptoms. Over the months, many things that people said and did brought comfort at various points, often when Suzanne needed it most, but the situation did not immediately right itself because she understood it more or knew that other people had been there. It was a comfort rather than a cure but alongside medical intervention it all helped to contribute to her recovery.

Once Suzanne came to terms a little with the diagnosis, she felt freer to tell people about it. For a few Sundays in church she burst into tears when anybody asked how she was. However, people were able to say things that reassured her because they now knew how she was feeling. Until this experience, she had assumed that depression would hit people with great problems and for whom life was tough, but she had a solid family and a supportive husband, good friends and a caring church. It came as a shock to realize that it can happen to anyone, regardless of their circumstances. She appreciated the extensive support structure around her and often wondered how people coped who were single parents or who had few around to support them. At the same time, it underlined the fact that all the support in the world would not necessarily prevent it happening.

Suzanne's church minister was an important part of that support structure and visited her regularly. Within the church there is a prayer chain where a number of people receive regular requests for prayer by email, text or telephone. When her minister first asked her if she would like her name added to the chain she hesitated because most other requests were for physical needs. Sometimes the requests were anonymous. If she put her name to this request it was going to be very public. Then she thought, "What is the point in keeping it to myself? If anyone else was going through this I would like to know so that I could help." She agreed to let her request go on the chain. On the very day that her name went on the list someone arrived with a gift and someone else invited her for tea. For weeks afterwards people in church asked how she was feeling. "It helped so much to know that people were thinking about me and praying for me."

Suzanne and Rick host one of the church home groups. They managed to keep it going even when Suzanne was at her worst because she found it a great support. Each time the group meets, there is an opportunity to ask for personal prayer. Once she was willing to be vulnerable, Suzanne shared her situation, asking the group to pray for her. This brought such a sense of comfort and support that she has continued to remind them of her needs, afraid that the effect of their prayers might somehow cease.

Her own prayers were difficult—they were mainly of the "please help me" variety. Her concentration was poor so praying or reading books or her Bible was difficult. She was adamant that she would keep going to church, feeling that it was something solid in her week, and being there with other people somehow helped and comforted her. She tried her best to concentrate through the sermon but her mind kept wandering off. She found this very difficult, having always been able to concentrate to read and study well in the past. Much of her day was made up of very short urgent prayers: "Strengthen me today," "Help me right now."

Suzanne had read in the past about people in difficult times feeling God's presence in a very special way but had never experienced it for herself. She heard people talk about hearing God's voice. How could you hear God's voice? How could you be sure it was not just in your own head? During the dark months after Daniel's birth, however, there were moments when out of the blue she suddenly felt calm. She could only put that down to God. In the middle of a very bad day she would suddenly feel "It's going to be okay. It will be all right." She would not describe it as peace exactly but it seemed to be a shaft of light that shone into her darkness for a moment, letting her know that the darkness was not complete.

Because she found walking helpful, she and Rick often walked round a lake near their home. On one particularly bad day at the lake, she began to feel that she was going mad, unable to control her racing mind. Suddenly she was aware quite clearly of the words, "I will never let you go." From that moment on, these words kept repeating in her mind, bringing a new sense of calm. Sometimes in all the worry and flurry when she felt as if her mind was spiralling out of control, she felt like shouting, "Stop! Help!" At moments like these she heard that response over and over again, "I will never let you go." No matter how bad she felt, she came back to that reassurance of God's arms being around and underneath her, holding her securely in the midst of her fear.

Suzanne still gets worried when she hears mental health issues discussed on television or radio because it reawakens concerns about herself. For now, she tends to turn off such programs, recognizing that she is still in the process of recovering and she does not need to increase her stress. A program or article about suicide, for example, affects her now because she knows something about reaching that point. She never actually wanted to end her life but she can understand how people must feel. She is haunted by the question, "Could I have got that bad?" That is when she remembers God's assurance that he will hold onto her, even if she feels she is slipping. "At times, I can feel as if I'm in a different world, totally absorbed in my own thoughts. I can feel anxiety and sadness creeping over me. Then Nathan runs into the room and I realize I've been out of it for a few moments. I realize I need to snap back into the present and go and talk to my children and come back into normality. I ask for God's protection over my mind every day. We don't do that often enough. I ask him to shield me from thoughts that would drag me down or make me anxious."

These days when Rick comes in from work and asks how her day has been, Suzanne still hesitates to say she has had a good day. "I would not exactly describe my day as 'good.' I'm still recovering. I continue to pray that the Lord will take the anxiety away from me and help me focus on the good things in my life. It does not happen immediately. I am learning to be patient, and to carry on in trust."

When Suzanne first went to see the doctor in July, he suggested that she should see a counselor as well as taking medication. The first appointment made her extremely uneasy as she and the counselor sat looking out of a window, talking in soft voices. She thought to herself, "This is it. I've gone over the edge. I've lost it. I can't believe I'm here. There must be something desperately wrong with me." The counselor's approach jarred with her as she encouraged her to reach inside and find the strength to help herself. In the depths of her depression, Suzanne thought: "But I can't do it myself—only God can give me the strength to cope." She decided that the counselor was on a different wavelength and was somehow putting an extra pressure on her that she could not cope with. She did not need more things to worry about. If she was going to talk to anyone she needed someone who was coming from the same perspective as herself.

In November, at her mother's suggestion, she decided to try a Christian counselor. The first time they met, Suzanne relaxed. She and Liz clicked instantly. Liz had been a midwife for years and had seen many people with similar symptoms to Suzanne's. That fact alone brought incredible relief as Suzanne realized she was not the only one to have felt like this. Her fixation on not being able to sleep had been a source of great worry to her as it seemed so abnormal but Liz had seen this many times. She explained to Suzanne that an obsession with one particular thing is often part of depression. The mind fixates on one aspect of life, whether it is sleeping, cleaning the house, or any of a whole variety of activities. Suzanne had been worried that the anxiety she felt was a separate issue—that even if the depression was cured she would still worry. Suddenly she was able to see it all as part of an illness from which she was slowly recovering and would one day leave behind completely.

Eight months after their first appointment, Suzanne still sees Liz every few weeks but the content of their time together has changed. These days they spend more time looking ahead and talking about the future. Suzanne is realizing that the perfectionist standards she sets for herself are not helpful. Slowly she is learning that having bad days or not having the house perfect all the time is acceptable. She still finds Liz a wonderful help. She says, "It does not feel like 'counseling' as such. It's more like just sitting chatting to a friend whose advice you can really trust. I feel very privileged to have her help."

Now that others know Suzanne's experience they feel freer to talk to her about what happened to them or to someone in their family. Suzanne says, "One thing I have come to realize over the past year is that peace of mind is one of the greatest gifts. A troubled, anxious mind interferes with everything else in your life. I'm not completely there yet. I still worry more than I should. I am much better than I was but I still get anxious about things. The difference now is that I feel free to share with others when I am not feeling so good and to receive strength and support from them, mentally, emotionally, and spiritually. I know that I am getting better. The important thing is not to suffer alone. If you are feeling low, tell a loved one and your doctor or midwife. Help is available and the sooner you obtain it, the sooner you will feel better. I prayed for God to heal me and he is doing that, but he uses a whole variety of different sources in the healing process. I had to be willing to be open to all of them."

**The eternal God is your refuge,
and underneath are the everlasting arms.
Deuteronomy 33:27**

6.

Restoring the Broken Places

"I've lost my faith," announced Eric. "I'm not going back to church."

Karen looked at him, stunned.

Her husband of twenty-two years was a church elder, house-group leader and sang in the worship group. She knew he had been going through a difficult time recently and had been acting out of character but she could not discover what was wrong. It rocked her world to think that the faith they shared was in question.

Until recently they had had a strong, happy marriage. As a twenty-year-old, Karen had married her best friend and over the years they had enjoyed doing everything together. Eric was very committed to his family and spent a great deal of time with the children. He was a devoted father and husband. Karen was grateful that they were such a good team. The children were growing up, with their eldest daughter now twenty and the other two children in their teens. They had reached a point in their lives where the children were more independent and, as a result, they had begun to spend more time doing fun things as a couple, having evenings out and weekends away. Life was good. From time to time there were the usual ups and downs that occur in any relationship but on the whole, they were happy and there were few arguments. To the outside world and to friends and family they were the perfect couple. Eric was well known and much respected in church and the community. This was the man Karen was going to spend the rest of her life with; they would grow old together. She loved him.

Over the last few months, however, the atmosphere had changed as Eric seemed to become more distant and cool. Up to that time there were no indications that anything was wrong, no arguments, no raised voices; he just seemed more preoccupied than usual and very tired. Occasionally he would be sharp with Karen but she put it down to him being under stress at work. She had no reason to consider anything else. She loved this man and trusted him. Gradually, however, the man she thought she knew became someone she no longer recognized. He began to show a hostile side that she had never seen before. This announcement that he had lost his faith and did not want to be involved in church life any more was a further cause of bewilderment. What was going on?

From that moment, Eric's behavior changed completely. He stopped going to church, refused to have anything to do with people from church, refused to talk to the church minister or go to counseling with Karen. At home a silent coldness replaced love and tenderness. He was unable or unwilling to explain what was happening. One day Karen, hardly believing she was saying the words, asked, "Is there someone else?" Vehemently he denied that this was the case. The following weeks were traumatic, with Eric threatening to leave and Karen pleading with him not to go. Desperately she hoped that this was some passing phase that would disappear and the husband she knew would be returned to her. He became totally remote, however, living in the same house but not communicating except for angry outbursts which are permanently etched on Karen's mind. She had never known such fear and rejection. The one who had been her closest friend, the person she knew best in the world was now acting like her worst enemy. She did not understand what was happening.

One weekend, Eric went to Glasgow on business. Things were so bad before he left that Karen spent the whole weekend wondering if he would come back. He reappeared at the end of the weekend but the situation did not improve. No matter how she tried, Karen could not reach him. One night he again threatened to leave. This had now become so routine that Karen did not believe he would ever do it. She knew he was very unhappy but he was such a devoted father that it seemed a totally ridiculous thing for him to even be suggesting. How could he live away from his children, where would he go? She saw his threats to leave as another way to hurt her rather than an intention to actually carry it out. At the same time, the situation was becoming impossible for everybody. She wept and prayed for God to somehow resolve the situation although she could see no solution. That night he took a quilt and slept on the sofa downstairs.

Next morning, Eric took their youngest daughter Christina to school as usual, kissed her goodbye, and left the family for good. Before he left he told Karen he would be back in the afternoon to collect his things. Deciding to avoid confrontation, she went to her sister-in-law who lived round the corner. When she returned home that afternoon it was to find that he had packed the car with his clothes and personal belongings and gone. He left his wedding ring in the plant pot where Karen found it later.

Karen was left to explain things to the children. She picked up Christina from school and brought her home. Sarah, the eldest, cuddled her little sister who was hysterical at the news. That was when the nightmare and pain really began for Karen. As a twelve-year-old, Christina was very close to her father and could not understand why he would leave them. She just wanted her daddy. She cried, "Mummy, make him come back.

You can make him come back." She was still at the stage where she thought her mother could do anything. Her older brother's reaction was different, giving the impression that he did not want to know anything about it. He expressed very little of what he felt at the time but his anger would appear later.

Karen will never forget the events of that day. "To this day I can recall those moments and the pain that engulfed our home. When a woman is betrayed by her husband, it touches something deep within your soul. It is an unimaginable grief to discover that the man with whom you have shared so much no longer wants you in his life." Karen found it particularly difficult to cope with the grief of her children, hardly knowing how to cope with her own. She wanted to shield them by hiding her tears and distress from them and yet she seemed incapable of doing so.

She was distraught. Her initial reaction was one of shock and disbelief that he had actually gone. In the early days she could not sleep or eat and found it difficult even to drink; she could not swallow without feeling ill. She was overcome by tiredness and grief. Soon she was caught in a cycle of being so tired she was unable to eat and because she could not eat she had no energy. This was exacerbated by countless visits to solicitors, meetings with barristers, and appearances at court to face the calculated reactions of a man she no longer knew. The pain seemed relentless as she was forced to accept the reality of what was happening. She could not believe that the husband she had known and loved over twenty-two years had actually walked out on them all. She could not believe that he could treat her and his children in such a way. She was convinced that there was more to it than him losing his faith—that would not make him leave them. She thought he must be having an affair but he kept denying it right up to the time he left, asking when she thought he would ever have the time.

Karen ached so much inside she thought she was dying. She thought of the saying "die of a broken heart" and decided it was true, it would be possible to die of a broken heart because there was a physical pain in her heart that blotted out the consciousness of anything else around. All she knew was the sense of rejection and sadness. All their adult lives they had been together and now she was alone. As time passed anger came too. The tragedy was not just that he had rejected her but that he had rejected his children. That was an unbearable pain.

In the six months after Eric left, Karen lost three stones in weight. Unable to eat at the beginning because of nausea and pain, she came to the point where she did not want to eat. Eric left just after Christmas. He was always very good about giving cards and presents, and as Valentine's Day approached in the month of February, she had this fantasy that perhaps she would get a Valentine card with a note inside saying that it had all been a huge mistake and he wanted to come back. She thought, "He couldn't not send me a card." Desperately she still hoped that he would telephone or arrive back on the doorstep, telling her how foolish he had been and they would kiss and make up. But Valentine's Day came and there was no card.

Karen was finding it increasingly difficult to cope with everyday life. She just wanted to get under a quilt and stay there and hope that sleep would take her away from the situation, even momentarily. She felt safe there, incapacitated as she was by her grief. She knows now that psychologically this had a disturbing effect on her youngest daughter who hated coming home from school to find her mother in bed. To this day Christina has a fear that surfaces if her mother is unwell enough to have to go to bed. While Karen was aware that it was upsetting for the family, she did not know what to do about it. The only way she could get through the day was to curl up and cry until she sobbed herself to sleep.

She used her decision not to eat as a way of getting back in control. She knew that she could not control her husband's behaviour or her children's grief and pain but this was one thing over which she had control. Somewhere at the back of her mind was also the feeling that if her husband saw how thin she looked and realized what he was doing to her then he would come back again. She got so low that she hardly cared what happened, until she thought about the children. What would happen to them if she was not there? They had already lost one parent, was she going to deprive them of another? She could not create a double loss for them. In the end they were her reason to go on living. It was for them that she had to get up and function in the morning.

A year after Eric left, Karen was at a low ebb. She was barely existing, trapped within a nightmare from which she could not wake. Each morning she would long for night to come and with it the hope of sleep to escape the pain. But there was no escape, just endurance. Eventually, realizing that she needed to get help for the children's sake, she went to the doctor who prescribed antidepressants during the day and something to help her sleep at night. Reluctantly she began to take them, in the hope that it might help her sleep pattern and that her appetite might return. She wishes now that she had taken the doctor's advice earlier as gradually the medication enabled her to think more clearly. In some ways it helped her not to fall off the edge altogether and enabled her to function enough to keep things ticking over at home.

The first two years after Eric left were the worst years of Karen's life. She thought she would never survive it and in her worst moments she did not particularly want to because there was no hope, no future and life was too painful to face. The grief she suffered at the ending of her marriage was a form of bereavement. The difference was that the torture continued by way of solicitors and continued court appearances where she was forced to come in contact with the person she once loved and respected but who now seemed a complete stranger.

The children's grief expressed itself in a variety of difficult and painful ways.

Christina was devastated by her father's departure and saw it as his rejection of her personally. She had great difficulty coping with the implications of his loss. Soon after he left she too became ill, unable to go to school, increasing Karen's despair. Ideally if Eric would return, they could all get back to normal. But she was powerless to win him back, powerless to make him love her, powerless to mend the brokenness of her family. Despite everything that Karen was struggling with herself, she had to find a way to try and help her daughter. She identified with her daughter's pain but felt helpless to alleviate it. The whole situation was becoming more and more traumatic. Desperately, wordlessly, she reached out to the God whom she had professed to trust when all was going well. Trust now seemed a totally different concept in this situation that was beyond her understanding or control. It was a grim holding on, despite all her questions, in the knowledge that he was the only one who could get them through this. Little by little, she began to do what she had to do and what she could do to help the family back towards some sense of normality. She was very aware that life would never be "normal" again. Recovery for each member of the family was a long, agonizing process.

Initially Eric kept in touch with Christina and would call at the front door to collect her and take her out for a couple of hours. If the two older children were at home he spoke to them when he called. In the first months after Eric left, their son Alan began to get very angry at his father's insistence that there was no affair while he was being seen in public with someone else. One day Eric dropped Christina off at home.

She came into the house and watched through the window while Alan went out to speak to his father. There followed a bitter altercation, witnessed by the neighbors, embarrassing for Karen and traumatic for Christina. The incident underlined for Karen the pain family break-up inflicts on the whole family.

About eighteen months after Eric left, Karen acknowledged that she had a major eating problem that she needed to deal with in some way. She tried to encourage herself to eat by gradually introducing foods that she liked and felt able to swallow. Instead of thinking of eating a meal she began to think, "What could I actually swallow that would go down easily and give me some nourishment? Perhaps a yogurt? Maybe a small bowl of cereal?" This was to mark the beginning of her return to better health as each mouthful of food nourished her body and began to renew her strength. Gradually, she began to take small steps back to normality. Step by painful step she began to feel better able to cope with the situation. As she began to eat, her weight loss became less severe and she began to feel slightly stronger, although the whole family remained very concerned about her. Even though she saw photographs of herself that fill her with horror now, at the time she could not take in the fact that she was too thin. She thought that her weight was fine although she knew that the children were very upset and could not understand why she would not eat. Gradually as time passed and the shock of the situation abated somewhat, she began to try for the children's sake to pick up her life again. It was three years before her weight returned to normal.

Although Eric denied another relationship to Karen, it was important to her that if she divorced him it would only be on the grounds of adultery. It was two years before he finally admitted that this was his reason for leaving. Karen will never know how long this relationship had been going on, although looking back at Eric's behavior with the benefit of hindsight, she can make an estimate. At one stage she desperately wanted to know all the details. She does not feel she needs to know any more. It no longer seems important.

At the time, she was unaware of the significance of the new interest in his appearance and phone calls from his workplace asking to speak to him, when she thought he was there. Because she loved him and trusted him there was no reason to question anything about his behavior at that stage. He was a highly respected Christian man. Karen and Eric knew that affairs were rife in his workplace and had talked together about things that went on there but Eric was the last person in the world that Karen would ever have suspected of looking at another woman. She could not understand his personality change but can now see how the pressure of another relationship and the struggle with his conscience and his faith could have caused the difference.

As Karen looks back to those days, she thinks, "How did I ever make it?" At the time she assumed her life was over. She was trying to deal with the trail of devastation that had been left, especially the misery and hurt of the children that was unbearable to her. She could see no time when things could be better. She realizes that other people helped her through when she was unable to do anything for herself. Some anonymously provided meals; some encouraged, prayed, and spurred her on. Some believed in her when she no longer believed in herself and convinced her she would survive. She relied on others to carry her—to think for her, to make decisions, to pray. She was physically unable to do any of those things for herself. When friends called to see her, she alternated between ranting at length at the injustice of life and having nothing to say at all, sometimes unable to lift her head to acknowledge them. Mostly, however, she needed to be able to talk, at the risk of boring people with her story, about what was going on not only externally but within herself. She needed to be able to tell someone how awful it was, how tragic it was, how painful it was. She says now that this had a huge part to play in her survival, as she was able to share her deepest feelings. There were a few very special people who listened and shared her journey, encouraged her and were not appalled by her strength of feeling, by the morbid thoughts that her life was over. Their loyalty, understanding and acceptance is something Karen will always treasure. However, it was God's enabling first and foremost that held her steady.

"There is much that has happened in my life that I don't understand and I have many unanswered questions. But I still held onto God. I don't think I would have come through it without the Lord. In the middle of the night, alone in my bed, he was the only one who heard the innermost groans of my heart and soul and at times I felt that he was all that I had. I have been too tired to pray, too tired to read, too tired to think, and all I've been able to do is hang on by a thread. I reached out to him without words. Others have done the praying for me."

Just before Eric left, Karen was getting involved in a voluntary capacity with an organization called Christian Listeners. The aim of this organization is to train people to listen more effectively to others. When Eric left, people said to her, "There's no way you'll be able to carry on with this—it will be too much for you." However, two weeks later, Karen took part in her first workshop. She remembers standing at the front in fear and trembling, not understanding herself how she was able to be there. She experienced God's enabling in an amazing way at that moment and that has been the story ever since. She says, "I remember little about those early days except an enormous sense of God's grace and enabling. I must have carried on in a trance-like state." Even at her lowest, she wanted to hold on to the call that she felt God had placed on her life to this work of listening to others. Because the training courses and workshops were booked and set up beforehand, she had to get up and go out and do what was necessary to run the event, no matter how she felt. At those times she experienced God's strength and empowering in an unusual way. Work was a physical way of proving God's help in a terrible situation.

With time, each member of the family has moved on to a certain degree of healing and acceptance. The intensity of the pain gradually decreased. Christina eventually picked up her education again, is now at college and has a job at the weekends. Karen herself is aware that her experiences have changed her and made her into the person that she is today. "It seems like another life now. I am not the person I was eight years ago. I am a stronger person, less fragile, more independent. I appreciate more what I have. I can see how God has really blessed me through my experience and has enabled me to come through a horrendous situation so that I have a life that is in some ways richer now than when I was married." This is true for the children also—they are different people than they were before the pain of their father's departure. The Bible verse that keeps coming back to Karen is from Jeremiah 29:11: "'For I know the plans I have for you,' declares the LORD, 'plans to prosper you and not to harm you, plans to give you hope and a future.'" At the time, although the verse seemed to be God's word to her, she found it very hard to believe while in the middle of the situation. "I remember looking at it and thinking, 'Where is the hope and the future in this? What possible gain can there be for anyone in this situation?' These words have stuck with me for as long as I can remember and they have become my cornerstone, to which I keep returning. And despite the tragedy of what has happened, I do believe them to be true."

Listening took on a new meaning for Karen as she herself began to experience the powerful healing effects of being listened to appropriately. She needed to talk over and over again as she tried to understand what had happened in her life, especially the things that were too hurtful for the children to know. Listening has played a significant part in her recovery. Her experience of being able to talk and to be really listened to has brought her to a place of peace and forgiveness.

"If you had asked me at the time if I could ever forgive my husband's unfaithfulness, and his abandoning of me and his children like something you would scrape off your shoe, I would have said no. But if I had been waiting to *feel* a sense of forgiveness towards him I would probably still be waiting. Forgiveness has been a slow process which started with the decision to forgive. I chose to forgive because I knew if I didn't it would eat me up inside and destroy me and he had almost done that already. I did it so that I could be set free. The feelings of forgiveness came much later than the decision."

Karen will always be sad at the loss of her marriage and the devastation it has caused to her family, especially the children. However she feels that Eric has lost much more than she has, even if he has not yet realized it. "Often with loss can come gain, and I have to say that despite the tragedy of it all, I have gained so much more than I ever dreamed possible. I would never have chosen the path that my life took, but it has led me to unbelievable riches in the form of a deeper relationship with a God who will never betray or reject me, who will always love me unconditionally, who will love and protect me and never forsake me for another. At the end of the day, when all is stripped away, when you come to the end of yourself, God is all there is. Now I really know that God is all I need."

Eight years later, Karen is now employed by Acorn Ireland, responsible for delivering and developing training for Christian Listeners throughout the country. God has enabled her to be involved in this ministry totally by his grace and power. More comfortable working with individuals than in front of a group, God called her out of her comfort zone when she started this work.

"He continues to call me to places I would rather not go and to do things I might otherwise have avoided. He has taken all the broken fragments of my life and gently crafted them back together again. The fact that he has chosen to take this weak, fragile, vulnerable woman and use her, is a testimony of what he can do. God has enabled me to continue with my work in spite of, and even because of, my circumstances."

Karen's healing has come slowly but steadily and God has used many varied ways to repair the broken places in her life. He provided her with the right people at the right time to walk the road with her until she could see the way ahead. He has healed her broken heart and made her whole again. The nightmare is over. Her tears and turmoil were just for a season, and in spite of her doubts and fears that it would never end, that season has now passed. In many ways it feels as if her life is beginning again.

"What an amazing God we have. He has brought me out of darkness into light. In the early days I would never have dreamt it was possible. Life is good again. Different but good!"

Looking back now, Karen can see that God has been able to bring positives out of her tragedy and she does not want to waste that opportunity. The ministry that she is involved in now is richer because of all the pain she has known. "God did not bring about this situation but he has used it to change me. I honestly feel now that I would not have so much to bring to the ministry if I had not been through all that has happened in my life."

She knows that she will never be the same again. Both she and the children have had to grow up. Her priorities and her perception of life have changed. She sees life as very fragile and very precious now. And with that comes the desire to cherish every moment. She also has an insight into a world of which she never dreamt she would be a part. Having often heard stories of others who were going through the trauma of divorce, in the past she tried to sympathize without ever really understanding the impact of divorce on a family. Since her own experience, she knows the powerful connection of being able to reach out to another, look them in the eye and say, "I've been there."

"My children and I have seen and felt things that no one should ever have to go through. But suffering knows no barriers. I also know that I would have no story to tell if God had not picked me up each time I fell."

Karen still has bad days, bad weeks even, and some of the old struggles still raise their heads from time to time. Being a parent is never easy, even when there are two, but it is even more challenging for one parenting alone. Over the years, the family seems to take it in turn to experience outbursts of negative emotion—fortunately not all at the same time. "It continues to be a work in progress. I haven't always known the best way to be of help and I know I haven't always got it right. Often I have simply wept and endured it with them."

Karen is very aware that she has a hope and a future that cannot be measured in good health, a strong marriage and a happy family. If it depended on those aspects, she would have lost hope a long time ago. Now she knows that no matter what comes her way, she need never give up because her hope and future in the Lord supersedes anything that this world can offer. She has an assurance that whatever happens, it is neither accidental nor coincidental. "God is rebuilding my life in ways I couldn't have imagined, just because he loves me. God is in the business of restoration."

Karen also needed to know that the pain, sorrow, and rejection would fade with time—that she would not always hurt so badly. And this is what she now shares with others.

"Whatever you are going through today—however deep your sorrow and your anger and your loneliness, you will get through it. A morning will come when you wake up and your situation and how you got there will not be the focus of your day. There will also come a day when you will laugh again, a real hearty laugh that comes from deep within you. And then the day will come that you will see your children smile and share a joke, and that is when you will really know that the healing has begun."

**Provide for those who grieve
in Zion—
to bestow on them a crown of
beauty
instead of ashes,
the oil of gladness instead of mourning,
and a garment of praise
instead of a spirit of despair.
They will be called oaks of righteousness,
a planting of the LORD
for the display of his splendor.
Isaiah 61:3**

7.

In Sickness and in Health

When Sharon Yardy started her degree course at Greenville College in Illinois in the fall of 1966, the last thought in her mind was meeting the man who was to become the love of her life. Having just returned from India with her missionary parents, vaguely aware that she was different from the other girls, she felt awkward socially, and somewhat inadequate for the challenge of college. Sometimes she took refuge with her older brothers and their friends in the college cafeteria. Unknown to Sharon, one of these friends, Tony Casurella, was interested in her from their first meeting. She had no idea that this highly intellectual student two years her senior would have any interest in a timid young freshman. When she eventually ended up talking to him alone one day, she expected him to get up and leave immediately but instead they ended up talking for hours. Oblivious to his intentions at first, Sharon was amazed when Tony began to pursue her with determination. Nine months later, at the end of that academic year, they got engaged. Sharon was eighteen and he was her first love.

During that summer, Sharon's mother, who had strict ideas about what was appropriate for a young Christian girl, allowed Tony to come from his home three hours drive away and visit on alternate Sundays, but not to stay over at their house. Undeterred, Tony wrote to Sharon every single day. Each day she would get home from her summer job, pick up Tony's letter, pull the dictionary off the shelf and take herself up to her room to study his long epistle.

Her sister was bemused. "Why would you date someone you don't understand?" she would demand.

Tony, a linguist, was conversant in twelve languages including Hebrew and Greek, although some he used mostly for academic research. Hard to understand or not, his romantic letters to Sharon won her heart.

Two years after their first meeting, when Sharon was still two months short of her twentieth birthday, they were married. For Sharon's parents it was the first wedding in the family and they wanted to give their daughter as good a wedding as they could. Her mother did most of the planning and made all the dresses for the bride and three bridesmaids. Tony's father had a minister friend who owned a cottage on one of the Michigan lakes which he kindly lent them for their honeymoon. As they approached this deserted cabin, Sharon suddenly panicked as she realized she was going to have to cook. She had never cooked before, coming from boarding school in India and from a country where cooking in any case was very different to that in the United States. Philosophically she decided she would just have to learn so they went shopping for groceries and she started to experiment. It made an interesting start to their married life but showed an important side of Sharon's personality. Rather than bemoaning the situation, she treated it purely as a practical issue to be resolved. It was a trait that would stand her in good stead later in life.

By this stage, Sharon had completed two years of her college course. Tony had graduated and was about to start a job as associate professor in English at the university in Illinois in the fall. Suddenly Tony felt that instead of taking up the university post, God wanted him to go to seminary to study theology. Although it was past the deadline for applications, Tony was accepted and their plans suddenly changed. The summer after they were married, they drove for eight hours to Asbury Seminary in Kentucky, arriving almost penniless and with nowhere to stay. A stream of miracles brought them an apartment, groceries to see them through the first week, and a few pieces of basic furniture. Tony did three years graduate school at the seminary and stayed on to teach Greek for a year. Sharon spent two years finishing her degree course before teaching elementary school for two years. Their student years meant juggling part-time jobs and living on a shoestring but it was a rich time of discovering more about each other.

During their first year together, the young couple realized that if they were to keep their relationship strong they would have to work on communication. At first when Sharon felt hurt by something Tony had done or said, she tended to lapse into silence. Very quickly she worked out that she needed to communicate better and earlier rather than withdrawing into herself. Tony was very good at letting her express her feelings, listening with the dignified graciousness that marked his personality. Learning to communicate in a positive way meant that Sharon and Tony discovered good conflict resolution techniques in their first few months together that became a pattern for their marriage. There were times when they felt anger and frustration like anyone else, but they learned to handle it without hurting each other, refusing to be drawn into name calling or raising their voices. Perhaps that was one reason the bond between them remained so strong.

From the beginning, their relationship was marked by a special romance that attracted the attention of others. While they were dating in college they were regarded as the "couple of the college." People loved to be around them because of the unique nature of their relationship. This remained true throughout their married life, although Sharon and Tony were often oblivious to it. Other couples reached out to them and were touched by the strength of their relationship. Couples who came to stay with them in their home were particularly impressed. God blessed them with this very special relationship and used it to encourage others. Perhaps Tony's Italian background came through in his romance as a husband; he was creative in showing his deep love for Sharon in a thousand ways, little touches when they passed, writing beautiful love notes, washing the dishes. They always found weddings very romantic and when Tony was not involved in the ceremony they would sit close, holding hands. Once, when they had been married for many years and had four children, he was invited to speak at a friend's wedding and referred to the deep joy of his own marriage. Turning to Sharon and looking into her eyes as though there was no one else in the room he said, "At every wedding I attend, I marry you."

Yet Sharon did not take the gift of Tony's love for granted. Despite his very deep devotion and commitment to her, she often questioned why this should be so. Pursued by insecurities from her boarding school days in India, feeling that in comparison to Tony she was not particularly gifted, she was totally unaware that her warm winsome personality attracted people to her. She says, "I never lost the wonder that Tony loved *me*."

Often she would say to him, "Why do you love me?"

Once he wrote a long letter in answer to her question, listing many reasons:

"You often ask me to tell you why I love you. Let me enumerate *some* of the things I appreciate about you:

- I love you because you are the Lord's and because that colors all you do, say, think, and are
- I love you because you are thoughtful of others
- I love you because you are an extraordinarily good mother
- I love you because you are self-giving
- I love it that you are a flirt—toward me! . . . "

Flirting was very much part of how they related to each other, with a look, a touch, a teasing email. Sharon says, "I flirted shamelessly with him. I was giving him the come-on the whole time and of course, being a man, he loved it!" It was a relationship with a tremendous amount of laughter and they deliberately kept it that way, teasing and having fun with each other. Sharon says, "I never doubted his faithfulness and steady love even though I did not always understand why he had chosen me. In my mind I never wandered from him in thought because we kept our love for each other alive. We both worked hard at keeping alive our relationship with God and our devotion to each other."

During his postgraduate studies at Asbury Seminary, Tony began to wonder if God wanted him to be a medical missionary. Sharon, trying to be understanding and supportive was nonetheless disorientated at the frequent changes in his career path. Although Tony was a brilliant linguist he also loved science and maths and in an attempt to keep all options open, took a pre-med course at the same time as his Masters degree in divinity. At the end of both courses he was undecided. He was offered two places—one to do a PhD in theology in Durham University in England, and one to study medicine in Loyola University in Chicago. Then came one of the biggest struggles the young couple had faced in their time together. How were they to know what God wanted? During the year leading up to the final decision they struggled to know God's will, having special times of prayer together but unable to find an answer. Looking back later they chuckled at themselves as a young couple, so gifted in many ways and yet unable to see God's will when he gave them a choice about the way forward.

The night before Tony needed to register for medical school they got into bed at his parents' house.

"What are you going to do?" Sharon was perplexed.

"If I'm not in bed when you wake up," said Tony, "I'll have gone to Chicago to register for medical school. If I haven't gone, then we'll be going to Durham."

Sharon woke up next morning to find her husband still beside her so they got up and started to make arrangements to fly to England.

By this stage, Sharon was pregnant with their first child. They flew to England with two suitcases, Sharon's sewing machine and Tony's typewriter. Once in Durham, Sharon started making maternity clothes while Tony took up his studies in the university. Despite enjoying theology and research, he found it hard to go into a hospital for a whole year after that, realizing that he had to put the dream of being a missionary doctor behind him.

With Tony's doctorate completed at Durham, he moved to Emmanuel Bible College in Birkenhead as Principal. By this stage they were expecting their third child. As the work there developed and their fourth child was born, they realized that this was God's place for them. For eleven years they enjoyed working with the students and staff there. Then gradually they began to feel their work in England was done. Stephan and Joy, their two older children, were now facing their teenage years and decisions had to be made about where they would complete their schooling and go to college.

Around this time there were indications that Tony was beginning to have some physical problems although they did not appear to be of great significance. His handwriting became very poor, to the extent that he would practice writing so that people could read it. Always very musical, he took piano lessons along with the children. At first he did well but then found he could not make any progress. He assumed it was because he was learning as an adult and gave up the practical work, continuing with the theory. He had a beautiful singing voice and was sought after to sing solos at weddings and special occasions. Now he would spend longer and longer practicing before a performance.

"My voice won't do what it's supposed to do," he would complain. At the time Sharon put these factors down to the stress of Tony's job but looking back now she realizes something neurological was going on.

In 1987, the family moved back to the States where Tony had been invited to take up a post as Professor of New Testament in Western Evangelical Seminary in Portland, Oregon. It was not an easy transition for any of them, but particularly for the older children. They knew nothing about Hollywood, about American television, about the dress or lifestyle of an American teenager. Sharon found herself identifying with her children as she relived her return from India all those years before. For the first year she did not get involved in church or work as she tried to help them adjust.

For the first couple of years, the focus was on getting the family settled in America and Sharon did not pay too much attention to the occasional problems exhibited by Tony. Gradually, however, she realized that symptoms were accumulating and becoming more obvious. His writing was continuing to deteriorate. His handshake became loose and weak. People began to say to Sharon, "Is Tony okay?" One day when Tony and Jonathan, their second son, came home from a game of tennis, Jonathan came into the kitchen to say privately to Sharon, "Mom, Dad kept falling today." Soon afterwards, Tony came in saying, "These shoes are no good for tennis. I'll have to get some proper ones." Sharon began to wonder what was going on.

People were beginning to find it harder to understand what Tony was saying and although at first Sharon and Tony put it down to his acquired British accent, gradually Sharon was forced to accept that she also was having difficulty. She began to say to him, "Tony, you'll have to enunciate more clearly," to which he replied with a grin, "No, you need to get your hearing checked." This became a family joke. One day Tony and the children had gone out to climb a mountain and Sharon was at home, working in the house, when the phone rang. A company called Miracle Ear was ringing in response to a request for an appointment for a free hearing test. Sharon's first response was indignant.

"No, I did not request an appointment. My hearing is perfectly fine."

Then, realizing that her teasing husband must be playing a joke, she changed her mind.

"Can you fit me in today for an appointment?" she asked.

Quickly she changed her clothes and headed into town for her hearing test. When she explained the standing joke to the practitioner, he co-operatively printed out a certificate stating that her hearing was fine, together with an invoice for $500. Sharon returned home and placed the certificate and invoice on Tony's desk.

Sitting around the table that evening, the family were all talking about their day together, the experience of the climb, and enjoying the meal that Sharon had prepared for them. Tony said, "And how was your day, Sharon?"

"Oh, mine was fine," said Sharon with a very straight face. "I did some work in the house and then I went and had my hearing tested."

Tony burst out laughing.

"You won't laugh when you see the bill on your desk," said Sharon. The laughing ceased abruptly. Money had been tight since they returned from England and every penny counted. It took a little while for Tony to realize that the joke was on him.

"That's how we dealt with it," says Sharon. "We laughed our way through some of the tough times."

It became obvious, however, that something serious was going on. Doctors agreed that there was a problem but were unsure what it was. As Tony's personality began to change, Sharon noticed that he found it hard to look people in the eye. Sometimes she would take his face in her hands and say, "Honey, look in my eyes." Later, before someone came to visit him, she would say to Tony, "Remember to look in their eyes and to ask about them."

Years later, Sharon would learn that part of Tony's brain that was affected by his illness controlled his relational ability but at this stage she struggled to understand what was happening. It was hard to accept that their wonderful relationship was being threatened by these mysterious changes. Tony, always so articulate, gradually lost the ability to express himself relationally without either of them understanding why. Sharon knew he still loved her but somehow things were not the same. In the end she knew it was his illness but it was a long, gradual, growing awareness. She never told him how this affected her, knowing that it would have broken his heart not to be able to put into the relationship all that he would have wanted to. At the same time, whatever part of his brain was affected, whatever the frustrations and problems of his illness, he always remained the same gracious, dignified Tony. He never became angry or difficult.

A series of tests began, exploring all possible psychiatric and physical problems. During the years of 1989 and 1990 they tried various alternative treatments including biofeedback. One theory was that toxic levels in Tony's blood were possibly due to lead poisoning but the extensive treatment for that proved fruitless. Some of the symptoms were similar to those of multiple sclerosis but again the tests for that were negative. They knew that lesions were growing on Tony's brain but they had no idea why.

Eventually, one day in 1993, they had an appointment with a neurologist who had been looking at all the test results. They were shown into a large impressive office and sat across the desk from this important man with all Tony's files in front of him. Gently he told them that Tony was suffering from Cerebellar Ataxia, a progressive degenerative disease about which very little is known. It is a disorder of the nervous system, with the cerebellum being the part of the brain that controls balance and co-ordination. In some cases it is not known what causes the condition. Eventually other parts of the brain as well as the cerebellum would be affected.

"How long do you think we have?" Sharon forced herself to ask the question.

"Probably two years."

They did not stay long in the office—there seemed very little to say. Tony remained his dignified and polite self as they said goodbye to the doctor. Outside, they sat silently in the car while normal life, amazingly, continued around them.

"What are you thinking?" asked Sharon, eventually.

"Eagle."

"Yes. Eagle."

From early in their marriage the eagle had symbolized for them the way to meet difficulties. They had heard that the eagle, knowing that a storm is coming long before it actually arrives, flies to a high spot and waits till the wind comes. Then it rises on the wind and uses the storm to lift it higher. Throughout their life together, Sharon and Tony had set their mind and faith on God. Now they were going to allow God's power to lift them above despair.

"Tony and I chose to soar above the storm," says Sharon. "Of course it's easier to say when you don't know all that you will have to go through but God gives strength in the day to day walk. That's what it means to 'soar on wings like eagles.'"

They returned home determined to make the best of their time together. Tony was still working at the seminary. Due to his lack of balance he was using a walking stick and he was finding it increasingly difficult to manage the stairs at home. Sharon realized that they would have to move house. It took her a long time to find the right house, one that would be suitable for Tony as his condition worsened. Eventually she managed to find the perfect place, with doors wide enough for a wheelchair and a deck opening out of their bedroom where she could put an exercise bike so that Tony could exercise outside when the weather was suitable. She had to have a few adjustments made to the bathroom, but soon the new house was ready for them to move into. She sent out invitations to a party on moving day, promising lots of laughter, exercise, and food. About forty people responded to the invitation and came along to help. Each family was responsible for moving one room from the first house to the second. Others were responsible for the garden and outside space. Teenagers who had come reluctantly, brought along by their parents, joined in and caught the spirit of it all. At the end of the day some of them said, "That was the most fun day of my life." It was a real example of God's people helping each other. The first week after moving into the new house, Tony started using a walking aid instead of a stick so the move had come just at the right time.

Trying to come to terms with the devastating diagnosis they had been given, Tony and Sharon set out to prepare themselves for what was to come. They read *Tuesdays with Morrie*[4] aloud together, lessons on facing the end of life, given by an elderly college professor to one of his former students on his Tuesday visits. They identified with Morrie as he dealt with his own degenerative illness and approaching death. Morrie decided to make the best of the time he had left, seeing himself as "research" from which others could learn and counting himself lucky to have so much time to say goodbye. They learned that Morrie gradually loosened his interest in some of the outside world, as newspapers and mail became less significant to him, and he focused instead on music and nature. When asked what he dreaded most about his slow, insidious decay, he said: "Well, Ted, one day soon, someone's gonna have to wipe my ass." When that point came, Morrie made the decision not to fight dependency but to enjoy it, looking on it as a return to childhood days of unconditional love and attention. Sharon and Tony looked ahead to such a time and talked about it together.

They moved on to reading *Living with the End in Mind*.[5] The focus of this book was on getting everything ready for the family so that life can go on as smoothly as possible for the rest when one member of the family goes. Sharon says, "We prepare for retirement and other things but not death. This book helped us to see this and to face it. Everyone around us was praying for healing but at a certain point we stopped praying for healing and prepared for death." After reading the book they made a living will which they both signed. Together they worked on the thanksgiving service that would be held after Tony's death. They put together a book of photographs and memories of his life entitled, "Heaven, here I come." They were working together towards his final days on earth and focusing on heaven.

Keeping track of the finances had always been Tony's area of responsibility rather than Sharon's. She was happy to keep to a budget but Tony, with his very methodical mathematical mind, looked after the finances in general. The year after they received the diagnosis, Sharon and Tony went together to the tax office as Tony was having trouble walking. To their dismay they discovered that Tony had made such a big mistake in their taxes that they owed $6,000. Such a situation had never arisen before. They had never in their lives owed anyone money. Taking a deep breath, they realized that they would have to find the money somewhere. Sharon worked extra hours and they scrimped and saved over the next year to pay back what they owed.

The following year when they went to see about their taxes they discovered that the debt was even larger—this time they owed $8,000. It was the only time Sharon ever cried in front of Tony because of frustration with his illness. They had always been so careful with money that to be in this debt for two years in a row was incredibly difficult. When she had stopped crying, Sharon gave him a hug and said, "I'm okay now." When they got home she decided she would just have to start again and pay back the debt. By that stage, Tony was unable to express emotion very much, but later Sharon would find an email he had spoken into his voice-activated computer, sent to his prayer partner: "I made mistake on taxes. Hard on Sharon. Please pray for her."

The second time that the tax mistake occurred, Sharon realized that she had been in denial about the way Tony's brain was being affected. At the time of the diagnosis she had asked the doctor whether he would be affected cognitively and he replied, "Of course not." Wanting to believe that statement was true, Sharon had tried to ignore signs that all was not as it should be but now she was forced to recognize that Tony's brilliant mind was being affected by the sinister force taking over his body. She realized that finance was one more responsibility she would have to assume. She was gradually taking over more and more control of everything. She was gaining all the power in the relationship and it was a power that she did not want. Instead of the togetherness they had always shared, she found that she was making decisions alone. Because they knew so little about the illness and had so little guidance about how to cope, they were just feeling their way and learning every day as they went along. Cerebellar Ataxia is a very rare disease—they only ever met one other person with the illness.

The walking aid allowed Tony to get from the house to the car and to go short distances unaided but for any further distance, going to the shops or out for a walk, he had to use a wheelchair. Sharon was becoming increasingly uneasy about the state of his elderly car. Although they were a two-car family, one was an old banger which Tony insisted on driving. Sharon, however, was concerned that if it broke down he would not be able to walk or get help. He refused to drive the better car, wanting Sharon to have it. Now in charge of the finances, Sharon came to a decision. She went out and bought a brand new car and had the salesman drive it to the house. When it arrived at the front door Tony was amazed.

"What's that?"

"That's your new car," she replied with a grin.

He drove it for two years after that and was able to put the walker in and out of it by himself, giving him great independence. Financially it was not the best decision Sharon ever made but she was taking care of him as best she knew how.

One Sunday lunch time, Tony shared that the students were having difficulty hearing him in lectures. Determined to help him keep working as long as possible, Sharon got up from the table and looked up the details of a sound equipment store downtown. Setting out for the store, they managed to find portable sound equipment that he could manage to take around on a trolley. Sharon went with him to the college and showed him how, by wearing a headset, he would be able to amplify his voice and continue teaching. Marking papers was also a problem, and as he became unable to use his fingers on the computer keyboard, they had found software that allowed him to operate it by speaking. That worked for a short time but not for long because although the software was designed to adjust to individual voices, Tony's voice was changing almost from day to day. Soon the software could no longer cope. This was the only time that Sharon saw him show frustration at the limitations of his illness.

As Tony gradually became more disabled, he and Sharon discussed how long he would be able to continue at the seminary. They agreed that it would not be fair to the students to carry on once it became difficult for him to do a good job. At one stage, he emailed his resignation to the college board but they refused to accept it replying that they needed him. He remained in his post for another six months after that. One day he suddenly announced, "I can't drive tomorrow morning." Sharon and their daughter Alison, who was living at home, both had full-time jobs but they quickly reorganized their schedules so that they could get Tony to work the next day. One week later he reached another stage in his illness when he left work for the last time.

Gradually, Sharon took over responsibility for more and more of Tony's life. As he became less able she took over his personal care, feeding, toileting, and dressing him, sorting out a week's supply of films for him to watch, organizing visitors and carers. Knowing how important his devotional life was to him, when he was no longer able to read his Bible she went out and bought a collection of devotional videos where inspirational nature scenes were combined with hymns and passages of Scripture. Then she discovered that a television channel broadcast similar programs, interspersed with a two-minute devotional, between midnight and 5.00 a.m. She stayed up all night and taped the programs for him, cutting out the adverts as they appeared so that he did not have them interrupting his devotions. She was able to build up hours of devotional material which she would play for him for half an hour each morning or evening. In months to come, when she was at work, carers would keep to the same schedule. Each evening, following a pattern that they had kept throughout their marriage, they prayed together, with Sharon vocalising the prayer for both of them as Tony became less able to speak.

It was an evolving illness and Sharon was aware that despite her closeness to her husband, she had no idea what it was really like for Tony. When they stood side by side as a young couple and promised to love each other "in sickness and in health" they never could have guessed that the future held an illness like this. No one seemed to fully understand what was going on but it was gradually affecting every part of his life—his ability to communicate, his emotions, his sexuality. Yet Sharon knew that underneath Tony was essentially the same person to whom she had made her commitment all those years before. When she was putting on a catheter for him, he would give her such a sorrowful look and Sharon would say to him, "You would have done it for me." She says, "It could just as well have happened to me and I would have needed love and care. He would have been faithful to me also. There was no question about what I would do and there was no option. The thing we had was very precious and lasted through the traumas of illness."

One of the early symptoms of Tony's illness was that his taste in food changed. Normally he loved meat and chicken but suddenly when Sharon put chicken on the table one evening he said, "I don't want chicken any more." At first Sharon was annoyed, thinking, "He has always liked chicken; how can he suddenly decide we're not going to eat it any more?" but then she realized that it was part of his illness. The situation kept changing each week and she began to wonder how she could keep up with it. Normally a very organized person in the house with menus and shopping planned in advance, Sharon felt disorientated by the constant changes. He began to cough while he was eating as swallowing became more difficult. Sharon did what she could to help him feed himself as long as possible although it called for constant creativity. She got him special cutlery that was easier for him to hold and found mats

that did not slip on the table. Giving him cut up food progressed into food that was mashed and soft. As his ability to
swallow declined further she began to liquidize everything,
from fruit to a full meal. It meant that when she was doing a
roast for the rest of the family, she would do a liquidized version for Tony. By this stage, unable to hold a cup, he used a
straw for drinking. Just planning and preparing his food
required great effort.

Sharon says, "Children develop and change and we don't
think about preparing special food for them as work or a trial
because of our love for them. Of course, we have the excitement of seeing them grow and develop as we care for them.
The process with Tony was the reverse of what happens with
a child because Tony was becoming more and more dependent but the love and the concept of caring that we had shared
so deeply over the years was still there." Eventually, Sharon
had to feed him everything.

From June 2000, Tony's condition deteriorated to the extent
that he could not be left alone. During the summer Sharon
was able to cope but by the time she returned to full-time
work with school opening again in September, Tony was
receiving hospice care at home. She drew up a rota for three
caretakers and herself so that over the coming months Tony
would have twenty-four hour care. Their youngest daughter
Alison, a trained nurse, gave up her job to be at home and
help care for him. Their other daughter, Joy, lived nearby with
her young family and took her turn to be there as often as she
could.

Tony talked a great deal about heaven, although in the final
months "conversation" came to mean grunts and groans from
Tony and then nodding as Sharon guessed the right word or
idea. Once he said to Sharon, "Do you think God will have a
bike in heaven for me?"

"You bet. He'll have the best. But he'll have a problem with you—you'll want to be so close to him, you'll be cycling round him all the time."

Tony laughed so hard.

"He'll send you off exploring to go and see your mother and all your friends."

Going back to work in September was challenging for Sharon as she was starting a totally new job as school counselor, alongside caring for her dying husband, and organizing carers. After Christmas she warned her employer that she would need two weeks off when Tony died but it was going to be difficult to find a substitute to cover her absence. "He won't die till you get a substitute," said Sharon.

One day at the beginning of April, Tony tried to communicate something to Alison and Sharon, making sounds and pointing at the window at the end of his bed.

"What is it, Tony?" Sharon began to list the possibilities. "Is it a bird? Trees? A cloud?"

Frustrated, Tony shook his head to everything she suggested. She gave him water, wiped his brow, went through the routine of all the things she normally did to help him feel more comfortable. Then she said to Alison, "Let's stop doing things for him and just sit here together." As they sat quietly holding his hands, Sharon had a sudden thought. "Tony, do you see heaven?"

A wonderful expression came over his face.

"Yes."

"Angels?"

"Yes."

He then struggled to sing in a voice that was almost completely gone: "I love you, Lord, and I lift my voice to worship you. O, my soul, rejoice."[6]

It was the last meaningful communication they had with him but it will remain with them for ever.

In the following days, he floated in and out of consciousness. On April 6, Joy telephoned Sharon at school.

"Mom, I think Dad is going to die soon and I don't want to be alone."

Sharon left school, telephoned the boys and stayed by Tony's side every minute as the end approached. Jonathan was at medical school in California and had spent his entire spring break two weeks before taking care of Tony in order to give Sharon and his sisters a break. Stephan, living in Kansas, was desperately wanting to say goodbye. As they waited for him to arrive, Sharon kept saying, "Honey, Stephan is coming to say goodbye to you. Just hold on." In between times, she was on the telephone for an update from the friend who was bringing Stephan from the airport. She had a chair waiting by the bed when he arrived and he had twenty minutes with his father before he died. It was April 9th, 2001, eight years since the initial diagnosis.

Five hundred people packed the church for the two and a half hour thanksgiving service and the meal afterwards. All four children participated in the service as well as a number of Tony's friends. Jonathan struggled with tears as he talked about his father, and true to the family's sense of humor, started to pull long rolls of toilet paper from his pocket. The whole congregation laughed while he blew his nose and continued. Tony would have appreciated the comic element. A PowerPoint presentation of photographs commemorated significant milestones in Tony's life. Some of his students sang his favorite song "Find Us Faithful" by Jon Mohr. He used to make Sharon listen to it and repeat the words to him.

The burial took place a couple of days later when the family and a few close friends took shovels and dug the grave themselves. It was something that Sharon felt she wanted to do and when asked, the children all wanted to participate.

Before leaving for the cemetery they went through the house and each one picked a flower out of the many flower arrangements to represent their own individual feelings. At the graveside they sang hymns, read some passages of Scripture, and then individually laid their flowers on the grave.

Sharon was left with an overwhelming feeling of gratitude for the depth of their relationship. It made Tony's leaving easier because she had those memories and no regrets.

"It's not the love you understand when you first meet. None of us as a young person has any idea what the future holds. We make a commitment without knowing what it will entail. As we trust him, God gives us the strength to live it out from day to day, for better, for worse, in sickness and in health. That is marriage. That is love."

Those who hope in the LORD will renew their strength.
They will soar on wings like eagles;
they will run and not grow weary,
they will walk and not be faint.
Isaiah 40:31

8.

A New Direction

Hilary Perrott's eyes light up as she shows me a book entitled *Personality and Prayer.*[7] "I think you'll find this very interesting," she says. "It opens up a whole new world when we operate according to the way God has made us." Hilary is sharing with me some of the secrets of the Myers-Briggs Type Indicator®, a personality inventory that has given her a new direction in life at a stage when many people are thinking of doing less rather than taking on new projects. "I can hardly believe that God has allowed me to do something I enjoy so much and is so much the core of the person I am," she enthuses.

In the year 2000, when her husband, Michael, retired from a prominent position as Director of Christian Guidelines, a Christian counseling organization in Northern Ireland, Hilary had already retired from her career as a legal secretary. Retirement, however, is not a word that you hear Hilary mention when you talk to her. She is too involved with her many interests and projects.

Like many people, Hilary wishes that she had had clearer career guidance as she was growing up. When she left school, conscious of a desire to work with people, she planned to go into hotel management, but with little available in the way of training, she compromised by doing a secretarial course. She ended up working with Professor Jessop in the Royal College of Surgeons in Dublin, and then in the Moyne Institute in Trinity College. Hilary had no experience of the medical world but she found the professor to be a delightful person, involved in a multitude of different projects. When she walked into his large room on the first morning, he looked at her, waving his arms vaguely in the direction of histology tables a foot deep in paper, and said, "Good morning, Miss Hewson, can you do something about all this?" Hilary, over-awed but determined, fitted quickly into the role of Personal Assistant. "I was known as 'Jessop's blonde,'" she says with a twinkle in her eye.

Then, one day she met Michael at the YMCA tennis club. Although mutually unattracted at first, the relationship gradually deepened. Eventually she abandoned Professor Jessop to marry Michael and live in the wilds of County Meath, where he was teaching in a Bible school. A year later they moved to Dublin, where Michael worked with the YMCA. For ten years he traveled extensively as an evangelist, which meant being away six months in every year, while Hilary stayed at home caring for their three boys.

As the children moved towards their teens, Michael and Hilary felt increasingly that they should change their lifestyle so Michael could be at home more with the family. This became possible in 1968 when he joined the staff of the Belfast YMCA, becoming first its General Secretary and then CEO. After fourteen years in administration, he moved sideways to the newly created post of Director of Evangelism and Counseling with the YMCA. The family ministry had begun.

Michael and Hilary had always enjoyed counseling together but now others joined the team and training began. The work grew steadily as many came to appreciate the service being offered, and by 1994 Christian Guidelines emerged as an independent organization.

The following year Hilary went to Waverley Abbey for further training, and as part of that course she completed the Myers-Briggs Type Indicator, something that was to impact the rest of her life in a way she had never dreamed. She describes it as "totally life-changing." It transformed all her relationships and gave her a huge feeling of relief that it was acceptable to be herself. In the past, an unhelpful aunt had made a practice of comparing Hilary unfavorably with her sister, leaving Hilary feeling constantly in her sister's shadow. "I suddenly realized that it was not a case of her being better than me—we were different but we both had a valuable contribution to make in our different ways."

The Myers-Briggs Type Indicator, or MBTI as it is usually known, is a personality framework that helps to explore our preferences for taking in information and making decisions. It looks at where we prefer to focus our attention and live our lives. Hilary began to understand that people's preferences were not necessarily right or wrong but just different. She realized that people could celebrate their differences and learn to depend on each other, complementing each others' skills. "For example," says Hilary, "Michael is my checker, and I am his ideas person."

She also found it helped her listening skills—communication is much easier when we appreciate the personality of the person to whom we are talking. "Everything hinges on communication," she comments, "whether we are talking with teens or toddlers."

Spiritually, Hilary feels it heightens her awareness of how God has made her and helps her in reviewing what she is doing.

Hilary came back from Waverley enthusing about the benefits of MBTI. Michael, always supportive, and thinking it would be of great benefit to many in Northern Ireland, suggested that she go ahead and train as a practitioner. His view was, "We can't take everyone to Waverley for their MBTI, but you could train and then bring it here." Unfortunately, as a professional tool it carried professional prices and in the Perrotts' financial position the cost of training was prohibitive. Hilary decided to forget about the training and just enjoy the benefits in her own life.

One day, while Hilary was attending a committee meeting, Michael was having coffee with a family friend. He shared with her Hilary's experience of MBTI and her great desire to train for it some day.

"Why doesn't she do the training now?"

"It's a two-fold problem—both time and money."

"Tell Hilary from me that if she can find the time I'll find the money."

Hilary came out of the committee meeting to find Michael with a wide grin on his face. "Guess what, your MBTI is paid for!"

Hilary was both excited and terrified. On the one hand, she was being given the possibility of doing something she really wanted to do but on the other hand, the course involved elements like inferential statistics which had not been considered a necessary part of a young lady's education when she was growing up. As for the time factor, Hilary reflects, "At that time, Michael was working all the hours there were in the YMCA, our three boys were still at home, Granny was living with us, I was working in a part-time job to help pay the mortgage, helping with the counseling side of the work in the YMCA and was also involved with the YWCA. There wasn't a great deal of spare time to take on a whole new project."

Hilary hesitated but eventually, in 1995, with Michael's encouragement, she took the plunge and started not just the course, but a whole new era in her life. She found it fascinating but difficult—particularly when she faced the bugbear of inferential statistics. Feeling rather like Joan of Arc going to the stake, she went off to what was euphemistically called a "study week" in Oxford. As she traveled into Belfast to catch the airport bus, she noticed that she had come without her watch, so she dashed into a shop and bought a cheap one to see her through the coming week. When she found her own watch further up her arm some time later she realized how nervous she really was about this new venture.

What happened next is an extraordinary example of how God prepares the way for us when we "step out of the boat" and dare to follow where he is leading. In Oxford, Hilary booked into a guest house which had been recommended and was within walking distance of where the course was being held.

On arrival, the landlady was very helpful.

"There is another lady staying here who is doing the same course as you. She said to tell you that she has a car and will be glad to give you a lift."

Hilary was grateful that she would have company on the first morning of the course, but still went to bed almost too frightened to sleep. When she came down to breakfast the next morning to meet her colleague she discovered that she was a Christian—and a mathematics teacher! Hilary says, "She helped me with the statistics, I helped her with the theory, and we have been friends ever since." Throughout this time, Hilary felt that God had his hand behind her, pushing her to fulfill her dream and that as she took each tentative step, he helped her to move forward in his plan for her. She found the course totally absorbing and was interested to note that about two-thirds of the people in her workshop were involved in Christian work. During the course, her sense of calling to MBTI was confirmed, as she realized that it fitted in exactly with the person God had made her.

The whole purpose of MBTI is to understand the needs of the individual—both personal and professional. The underlying philosophy is clearly that we are all individually crafted, and when nature is combined with nurture, there simply is no one else with the same mix in the world. It underlines our uniqueness. Hilary says, "There is no one else who can be what God wants me to be or who can do what God wants me to do."

Setting up MBTI as a business on her own was a big challenge for Hilary. She had nothing with which to compare it, as it was not widely practised in Ireland at that time. Despite being trained and qualified, at first she felt she did not have enough skill in how to present it, and home pressures made it difficult for her to get time to explore it in more depth. It was a new idea to most people, making marketing a challenge. To begin with she offered the Indicator to some clients free of charge, and gradually word spread as people were impressed with what they experienced. Her case list is now in the hundreds.

For many people, mid-life brings the realization that they are square pegs in round holes. Some have a dream tucked away at the back of their mind, postponed or ignored for years, because the time or opportunity to follow it has not seemed possible. Suddenly Hilary realized that helping others through MBTI could change life for them too. Her personality, the way God had made her, gave her a desire to help others see the benefits of MBTI in their own lives.

At a masterclass in Oxford one day, Hilary was sitting with a lecturer in pastoral theology from a Bible college in England, and asked him a question that had been bothering her.

"What do you say to people who think that if you have the Bible you don't need this stuff?"

"Well," he replied, "we find that where the rubber hits the road, this helps you put the Bible into operation."

Hilary quickly discovered in her own life and in the lives of those she worked with how God can use MBTI to show us who we really are and why he has made us as we are. She says, "It enhances our Christian walk and effectiveness. It really works. I wouldn't be bothered putting this much effort into it if it didn't. It gives us tools for living. But how well it works is up to the individual, how much they take it on board and how much they use it. I give people as good an understanding and as practical an application to their individual lives as possible. It's up to them what they do with it."

One of Hilary's clients was the late Revd Howard Lewis from Belfast who did the Indicator when he was in his fifties. His reaction was, "If I had done this thirty years ago my whole life would have been different." One day, when Hilary gave a brief MBTI taster, someone borrowed a book from her about the interaction of personalities in relationships. She returned it to Hilary some time later with tears in her eyes, saying, "If I had had this earlier my marriage might have been saved." Responses such as these give Hilary a great sense of fulfillment knowing that she can have a part to play in helping people realize their potential.

The more she began to use MBTI, however, the more she realized how much there was to discover. Depth and breadth of experience came as she used it with clients and talked about her experiences with other trainers. Her goal is to build on the knowledge that clients already have. "I'd love to get small groups of people together to discuss the implications of their MBTI and to take things to a different level. It can be very helpful to apply professionally, personally, and spiritually," she says. Her eyes sparkle with enthusiasm. "I find it the most enormous privilege to have this level of personal interaction and see people free to develop into what God meant them to be." She is energized and excited by the opportunities before her.

As Hilary helped people recognize their strengths, she realized afresh that any strength overused can also become a liability. MBTI encourages us to play to our strengths and she freely admits that at times, as a result of her passion for people, she has overstretched herself. She now tempers her use of MBTI with advice on keeping a healthy balance in our lives. "Personally I have had to discover that the only shoulders broad enough to bear the pain of the world are Jesus' shoulders. I can't possibly take the world's pain on my shoulders and if I try to do so then I can't function properly," she says.

Although MBTI was an exhilarating new venture for Hilary, it was never going to be her top priority. Throughout her life, family has come first for her, meaning that her work with MBTI is done rather spasmodically. "MBTI could be totally absorbing but it would not be right to let it become more important than the family," she says. She began to use it more as the family left home and their needs became less pressing. If her priorities had been different, she could have used it much more remuneratively in the commercial world. But her real vision is to see it used in churches. She would love to see the potential of the Indicator utilized in the Christian community with more people aware of their own and others' special gifts and abilities. She continues to work towards that end.

These days she and Michael support each other in the new roles they have each undertaken in retirement—Michael in writing and Hilary in MBTI. Family is still a priority even though the children have grown up and left home. Two of their three boys now live in London, and one in Northern Ireland. As the boys set up their own homes, Hilary felt that it was important to be available without being intrusive. There were times when she had to accept and understand that they needed to resolve their own situation and that help was not always necessary. She also keeps in mind the fundamental MBTI principle that when they operate differently from her, it is not necessarily wrong, just different. When she thinks she may see a solution to a difficulty she will sometimes say,

"Have you tried...?" With both children and grandchildren, Hilary tries to put suggestions in the form of questions rather than statements.

"Is there any ironing you would like me to do?" is an offer she often found gratefully received. One day, she arrived to find one of her daughters-in-law doing a huge pile of ironing for a neighbor who was unwell.

"Are you doing that on top of all your other commitments?" asked Hilary.

"Yes, just the way you did it for me," was the reply.

She has five grandchildren, between the ages of eleven and eighteen. "The middle one is sixteen and at the stage where everything is 'boring,'" laughs Hilary. When her first grandchild was born, her son was putting huge efforts into setting up his own business, and the young couple had demands upon them which gave the grandparents many opportunities for childminding.

"Grandparenting is a huge joy," says Hilary. "You have most of the fun and only some of the responsibility." As more grandchildren came along she developed a strategy, to be available most but not all of the time, helping as much as possible but recognizing that she needed to think about herself too. "We are told by Jesus to love our neighbor as ourselves. Sometimes I have been guilty of forgetting that little word 'as', forgetting that I am supposed to consider myself too. All of us who are mothers or grandmothers or who are involved in caring for others in any way need to be conscious of this. It's a constant challenge to keep a balance in our lives and not feel guilty about looking after our own needs. We can only be useful to others when we are caring for ourselves too."

As our children grow, our role changes from that of a parent to being a coach and a sponsor. Hilary had a good role model in her own mother who once said to her, "I never expected you to like what I like." As a young mother, that gave Hilary a sense of freedom which was invaluable in her family life, and meant that they could all have fun together without feeling judged or inadequate. She is very conscious of her mother's words now when she looks at some of her teenage grandchildren's clothes or hears about their lifestyle. She recoils with horror at the thought of saying, "It wasn't like that in my day." She tries to keep in mind that culture is constantly changing and not set in concrete. "It is God's world and he keeps it on the move. He is in control of all the changes that are happening and they can be used for good and for the kingdom. It is important at this stage of our lives that we keep looking forward, not backwards, and have an open mind to adjust to change as it happens. We need to embrace it and see potential and opportunity."

Hilary feels strongly that it is not her responsibility as a grandparent to make decisions regarding her grandchildren. "Parents have to take calculated risks with their children. Naturally I am concerned about my grandchildren's well-being but I don't allow myself to worry about them. I pray for them and then leave it with God. I let the parents do the worrying!" At the same time she is conscious of the challenges young people face in today's world. Parents can have rules about computers being in a common area where anyone can see what is being accessed online, but with the privacy of iPods and other rapid technological advances, she is aware that parental control is not easy. She makes the most of any opportunity she can to help build a godly conscience in her grandchildren, with no topics barred. Her hope is that as they watch television or access websites online they develop that basic inner knowledge of right and wrong for themselves. Parents decide the policy for their own children but as a grandmother, she is interested to see how this varies from one family to another.

"I would like them to understand that I don't know it all. I've learned a few things along the way but this is their world and their life. I cannot live it for them but I love them no matter what. As little children they knew some behavior would disappoint me and now that they are growing up I hope that awareness is still there."

When the grandchildren were small, Hilary enjoyed whatever activities were important to the children at any particular stage, whether that was hearing about football or ballet or attending concerts and events in which they were participating. One granddaughter was very creative as a child so Hilary enjoyed taking her on shopping trips to buy ribbons and lace and creative bits and pieces. As they grow she works hard to keep points of contact with each of the five grandchildren. This is not always easy, but rather than giving up, Hilary makes a determined effort to keep the relationship alive. "The important thing is to enjoy your children and grandchildren at whatever stage they are—each stage passes very quickly."

These days, most of her grandchildren lead busy teenage lives and Hilary finds it takes more effort and ingenuity on her part to keep in touch with them. She tries to use a medium that is comfortable for them, which usually means email and SMSing, but she does whatever it takes to make it happen. Asking their opinion forms a useful bridge with them. One teenage granddaughter is doing a beauty course so Hilary took her makeup drawer along and said, "Can you help me sort out this muddle?" She has recently set a challenge for her fashion conscious granddaughters in London—she is going to put herself at their disposal for a Saturday to "dress a granny." "The only condition is that the result must be acceptable to both them and me," she says.

With her background in counseling and MBTI, Hilary knows how important it is to remember that each grandchild is different, and to take time to listen to them individually. She is prepared for their candidness.

Once, she was showing her recently taken passport photograph to Kathy who was nine at the time. "Granny, when you had that taken, were you very tired?" asked her granddaughter.

On another occasion her young grandson was upset about something his parents had done. "It's not fair, Granny," he complained.

"Let's sit here on the stairs for a minute," said Hilary. Gently she talked him through the situation and explained, "Life is not fair. Things happen in life and parents and those who love you cannot always fix them for you. Unfairness is something that happens to all of us all through life." Hilary's hope is that as she enters into the concerns of her grandchildren now, she is helping to lay a foundation for understanding the bigger issues later in life when they experience greater unfairness. Another granddaughter was distraught when she learned that her best friend was moving abroad. "But I prayed about it so much, Granny," she said tearfully. This was the opportunity to talk about the importance of prayer, not as a slot machine with automatic answers, but as a relationship with God. It is a lesson that her granddaughter will continue to learn as she grows.

Hilary is conscious that she has opportunities to share with her grandchildren in a different way from their parents. "We never get a second chance as parents but we get a second perspective as grandparents. We can enjoy grandchildren without being under so much pressure. We may have input into their lives—'may' being the operative word. It is not a right or a demand." Hilary keeps in mind that at different ages the grandchildren are at different levels of understanding but she tries to be frank and able to have open conversations with them, discussing any topic at the meal table. She has said to them, "If I hear of someone talking about sex as 'it' I know that's all it is—there is no relationship or intimacy there. Sex is meant to be much more than that."

One thing that Michael and Hilary found was much appreciated was their offer to have the grandchildren stay overnight so that the parents could regularly have time alone. "It was also good for us as grandparents and grandchildren to have that special time together."

Alongside giving time to the family, Hilary continues with her other interests, including playing an active role on the YWCA board in Ireland as it re-examines the way ahead.

She keeps herself fit using an exercise video, and also does Pilates. She has discovered that she functions better on two meals a day rather than three, taking only liquids in between. "It just means I feel better," she says. "God designed me as a size twelve—just look at my frame and height—and for years I was more than that. I carried weight I didn't need to. Nowadays I try not to eat more than I need. It is all part of the concept of the whole of me belonging to God."

In the summer of 2004, Michael's brother and sister both died inside one week. This inevitably had a considerable effect on Michael and Hilary. They radically reassessed every aspect of the way they lived, what they had, what they did, how they used their time. They came home from the second funeral to sort out the attic and garage. They went through every cupboard and shelf in the house and got rid of all the extra clutter—keeping only what they use or enjoy. Hilary was never a hoarder but she makes it a habit to declutter more often now. "Sort and simplify is the rule," she says. She does not have a large wardrobe, but had a color consultation done to find out what suits her best and how to make the various items of her wardrobe work well together. She enjoys making the most of the items she has.

Hilary remains very involved in her local church which she loves. She is enjoying her new laptop, a necessary addition as the volume of work has increased. And she and Michael take time to enjoy life together, walking near the sea where they live, going out for coffee now that they have time to do it, and following their latest interest of ballroom dancing. "It's great fun," she explains. "It gives us both exercise and relaxation, although it also demands total concentration for an hour and a half. It's a great opportunity for couples to have fun together and brings a balance into our lives. When we get that right we are more effective and much happier. Rechecking my interests and output helps me see if I am leaving enough time and space for myself. Having the gift of enjoying doing several things at once, I have to watch that it does not get out of hand. Working smarter not harder is a lesson I am constantly relearning."

Hilary's interests have changed with the different stages of her life. Her previous interest in redesigning and planting gardens has now faded into the background rather than being a main focus. She used to enjoy embroidery, knitting and crafts of various kinds, but now prefers to focus on more people-creative things like MBTI. She has a pact with some friends about Christmas and birthday gifts because she has reached a stage where she does not want anything else to dust or water. Instead of buying gifts, they go out for lunch or coffee, alternately choosing places of interest, and savoring the time to enjoy each other, sharing joys and sorrows. She enjoys sun and warmth, color and music, current affairs, doing crosswords and observing human behavior, whether in real life or on television. To maximize her energy, she finds it helpful to change gear from tough tasks to the "fun factor" and to switch between using mind and muscle. She also enjoys power napping which she has the ability to do anywhere anytime. She has a list of things she would like to attempt, including learning to speak really idiomatic French and brushing up on her tap dancing.

"I disregard the numbers in birthdays," is Hilary's mantra. Certainly this vibrant woman has a great deal to teach us about what is sometimes referred to as "the third age." Her refusal to retire gracefully but rather to grasp this stage of life as a new opportunity and a new direction is a challenge and encouragement. Hilary says: "I realize now that no time is to be taken for granted. Each day is a gift and we must learn to value it. I never see what I choose to do as being prescriptive for anyone else. This is what works for me at present but God's plan for me next year (or next week) may be entirely different." Hilary is a walking example of what D.L. Moody meant when he said, "Preparation for old age should begin not later than one's teens. A life which is empty of purpose until sixty-five will not suddenly become filled on retirement."[8] Hilary is far from "old age" but her attitude to life ensures that the years ahead will be as consistently filled with purpose as those in the past and present.

It is exciting to realize at each stage of life that God still has a plan for us to fulfill and a task for us to do. We have no idea of the wonderful blessings he has in store for us. "No eye has seen, no ear has heard, no mind has conceived what God has prepared for those who love him" (1 Cor. 2:9). Any new direction brings challenges, but as God leads us forward he provides the resources that we need. Most of us use only a fraction of our true potential—often because we are afraid of failure. Are there things you have wanted to do but have never had the time, opportunity or perhaps the courage to try? Focus on your potential rather than on your limitations. We underestimate our capacity for change. There is no limit to what God can do through a life totally available to him. Erma Bombeck says, "When I stand before God at the end of my life, I would hope that I would not have a single bit of talent left, and could say, 'I used everything you gave me.'"[9] If God has placed a dream in your heart, it is there for a reason. Trust him and follow your dream, use your talents and become the person God wants you to be at this stage in your life. The late Selwyn Hughes used to say, "Never stop creating."

The question that faces each of us today is simple: "What does God want me to do? What is his plan for me today?" When we ask that question, really meaning it, we are often amazed and delighted by the answer—but be prepared for a shock too. God may have something more exciting in mind for you than you ever dreamed possible. Step forward and grasp it—he equips us for the task to which he calls us. In his strength you can be vital and creative as you follow the new direction that he sets before you—even, or perhaps especially, in retirement.

**See, I have placed before you an open door
that no one can shut.
Revelation 3:8**

9.

Finishing Well

I was struggling to read a huge red hardback edition of *Alice in Wonderland*. Knowing my love of books, Auntie Jean had given it to me the day before. I was mesmerized by the heaviness of the tome in my small hands and the excitement of the unfolding story. Auntie Jean always knew the best presents to buy. Recently, she had bought me a bookcase for my bedroom, in which to keep my prized books. Upon arriving to stay the following weekend, she took a look at the bookcase and said, "I must congratulate you on the way you have your bookcase organized." I glowed with pleasure. To please Auntie Jean was the height of happiness for an eight-year-old.

Because Auntie Jean lived alone, working during the week as a health visitor, she spent most of her weekends with us. Coming home from my music lesson late on a Friday afternoon was always marked by the excitement of wondering if Auntie Jean would be there when I got back. On her arrival, mysterious gifts would fall out of her overfilled car as she opened the door. Books, puzzles, exotic food that we had never seen before, clothes, hair ribbons, tubes of toothpaste and toothbrushes accompanied by some thoughts on dental hygiene—there was no end to the ideas that would strike her during the week, and accompany her to our house at the weekend.

We lived on the north coast of Ireland and outings with Auntie Jean often involved the sea or the beach. On one occasion, although a non-swimmer herself, she took us as children on a boat trip to the Skerries, a string of small islands off the coast. There are photographs of us all clambering cheerfully over the sloping seaweed-covered rocks, oblivious to fear or danger. Long walks along the beach were a regular part of her visit, with instruction on, and demonstration of, exercises on the beach and deep breathing of the fresh sea air. Being the eldest of the family, I was often singled out for the special privilege of a walk alone on the beach with Auntie Jean, where, as I grew older, our discussions included the love of literature that we shared and many philosophical and theological questions. She was a visionary, an idealist, and single-hearted in her devotion to God. These conversations were to remain with me in years to come and some to this day.

On Monday morning, Auntie Jean would return to work and take us to school on the way. For some reason we were always late when we were with her. Undismayed, she used the journey to impress on us the importance of studying well, of making the most of our opportunities, of having good friends, of washing our hands before we ate lunch, and any other inspiration that happened to come to mind. Before we got out of the car she would open the glove compartment, delve around among packets of tissues and tubes of hand cream and fish out a large bar of chocolate. "Keep your blood sugar up!" was her parting remark as she waved cheerfully, revved the engine and took off with a roar from the school gate.

Once a year there was a Sunday school outing to Belfast zoo. Because Auntie Jean taught Sunday school in our church, she and our mother both came with us on this annual event. The excitement lay partly in the journey itself—it was the only time we ever traveled by train. When the experience of the zoo and the fun of the pedal boats on the nearby miniature lake began to wane, we would take the bus into the centre of Belfast to visit the large department stores. There Auntie Jean delighted in buying a present, often a new dress, to mark the occasion. On the journey home on the train she would go over the events of the day and ask, "How did you like that? Did you really enjoy it?" Our reassurance that the day had been the best in living memory was all that she needed to go home content.

Christmas was not complete unless Auntie Jean was there to share it. She arrived on Christmas Eve, the car stacked to the roof with goodies, food, and gifts of all descriptions that we were not allowed to see, although excitement led her to drop mysterious hints as to what Christmas Day might bring. It was Auntie Jean who helped my parents pack pillowcases for each of us—there was no way a stocking could cope with her generosity—and then sneak them up the stairs to our rooms without disturbing us when we were sleeping. Long before morning we woke, and with great excitement, sat around on the floor to open our presents. Auntie Jean, delighting in the fun of it all, joined in the flurry of torn paper, noisy toys, and beautiful books. My more practical mother put on the kettle and served us all tea and toast as the initial excitement began to abate. She also took the opportunity to switch on the oven and start the slow cooking of the turkey, the aroma of which gradually permeated the house before breakfast time. Eventually we submitted to the necessity of going back to bed, often tucked in contentedly beside Auntie Jean, with a new book and a bar of chocolate.

Auntie Jean was an essential part of my childhood. Her influence upon me was profound. Her Christian faith was so much a part of her that I clearly understood from an early age that her concern for others and her generous nature sprang naturally from her love of Christ and her desire to be like him. I remember once opening a Bible in her house and finding inscribed inside it the words: "To dear Jean, in whose life I first saw Jesus." Sometimes I would travel with her in the car as she visited people in her district. The children in some of those country houses greeted her with almost as much enthusiasm as we did as her nephews and nieces. "Mummy, it's the nurse, it's the nurse!" they would shout as they raced into the house. Whatever the situation, she brought a sincere smile and a warm concern that reached out to everyone and radiated the love of the Savior she served. Her somewhat erratic driving was accompanied by the singing of some of the older hymns that expressed her faith so clearly—I often sat beside her in the car while she drove along singing "My Jesus I Love Thee" and "Jesus Keep Me Near the Cross". Once we met an elderly gentleman to whom Auntie Jean introduced me as her niece. Looking at me over his glasses he said, "Well, if you're as good as your Auntie Jean, you'll do." Without fully understanding what he meant, I knew that was exactly what I wanted to be.

These days Auntie Jean is unable to take me on outings and introduce me to her friends. For the last ten years she has suffered from Alzheimer's disease. Thanks to her medication she still knows me, although the circle of people she now recognizes is rapidly shrinking. Because of the tireless devotion of her husband, whom she married later in life, she was able to continue to live at home for nine of those years, but her condition is now rapidly deteriorating. She remains, however, my greatly loved and admired aunt and I know that the disabled body and mind which others see is not the person I know behind the outer façade. I look up above her chair to the photograph of the pretty young nurse that she was, with perfect skin, a glowing smile, and a twinkle in her eye. Her faith in God is still strong. Despite not knowing the day of the week or where she is geographically, she can complete from memory almost any psalm that is read to her. Her favorite is Psalm 91: "He that dwelleth in the secret place of the Most High shall abide under the shadow of the Almighty" (KJV). At a recent family gathering, she began to quote it to a room full of people who listened spellbound, more than one of us with a tear in our eye. She repeated the whole psalm word for word—in the King James Version of the Bible which she has used all her life. In the frightening confusion of memory loss, she still remembers the Bible passages that she learned as a young girl, even more precious to her now that so much around her seems unfamiliar.

The fact that she is eighty-five years old holds no meaning for her. Recently she said to me, "I wouldn't like to live to be too old. I wouldn't want to be a burden to anyone." She is unaware that she can do almost nothing for herself. Eating is a chore to which she submits reluctantly; her most often repeated sentence is, "When are we going to get tea?" but when it comes it is either too hot or too cold and is mostly left in the cup. Fastidious about her appearance throughout her life, she now has no appreciation of what she is wearing, dependent on others for her dress and personal care. When I do her nails she will sometimes look at them vaguely and say, "Are they all right now?" She has lost all sense of humor and anyone telling a funny story in her vicinity will be cross questioned in depth about the details as she struggles to understand why people are laughing.

The present is confusing for her and even the past is becoming cloudy now. We used to be able to reminisce together about her weekend visits when we were children, about Christmas and the Sunday school outing. These days, although she enjoys listening to the stories of what happened and even smiles a little as I talk, she wrinkles her brow at the end and says resignedly, "I don't remember." I say, "You were very good to us, Auntie Jean. We all loved you. You were like our fairy godmother. You were a great influence on my life." She seems pleased and says, "Was I?"

No one knows exactly what the future holds for Auntie Jean as she nears the end of her life's journey. One thing I do know, however, is that she approaches this stage of life with her faith in God stronger than on the day she first trusted him as a teenager almost seventy years ago. When I tell her I am speaking at a meeting she says, "Tell them they need to know the Lord. That's the most important thing." Sometimes she says, "What will heaven be like?" I say, "I'm not sure about the details, Auntie Jean. What do you think?" She replies, "We'll be with Jesus."

As a teenager, I remember looking at middle-aged Christians around me with a horror of settling down into what I perceived as an apathetic, mediocre type of Christianity. I was delighted when I came across Proverbs 4:18: "… the path of the just is as the shining light, that shineth more and more unto the perfect day" (KJV) or as the New International Version puts it: "The path of the righteous is like the first gleam of dawn, shining ever brighter till the full light of day." In other words, the initial enthusiasm of our faith does not have to diminish as we grow older, but instead can grow stronger and brighter. I resolved then not to be content with a half-hearted faith, but to aim to know God in an ever-deeper way as my life progressed. As I look at Auntie Jean now and admire the faith that has remained strong through all the joys and sorrows of her life, I long to reflect him to others as she has done and to grow more like Christ with every year that passes. It inspires me to see her faith shining brighter as she nears the end of life and approaches "the full light of day."

"It is the glow within that creates beauty. People are like stained-glass windows. They sparkle like crystal in the sun. At night they continue to sparkle only if there is light from within" (Bonnie Green).[10] Auntie Jean has always had that "light within." She sparkled when I knew her in the sunnier days of her life. Now in darker times, she continues to radiate the confidence that comes from a close lifelong relationship with her Savior.

Margene is also approaching the final stage of her life. I met her recently when I spent some time in Colorado. At fifty-four years of age, she faces death with surprising equanimity. Perhaps it is because of the closeness to God that she has experienced throughout the long years of her illness. "My grief is not for me but for all you who have to stay behind," she says. "I get to be with Jesus."

Margene grew up in what she calls a "dysfunctional family." Her mother was mentally unstable, but her father never really understood the problem, and not being very connected to the family, was unaware that the children were suffering emotional abuse throughout their formative years. Margene spent the summers with her Christian grandmother, who was quiet about her faith but lived out her close relationship with God in front of her grandchildren. At the age of sixteen, Margene committed her life to Christ, and as a university student, met Tom who was also a committed Christian. When Tom joined the Air Force, they continued their relationship by letter. One day, Tom telephoned and asked her to marry him. She graduated from nursing school on a Wednesday and got married the following Saturday.

As a child in her grandmother's house, Margene felt that God wanted her to go overseas as a missionary, so she was delighted when Tom told her that he felt God's call on his life and his decision to go to seminary to train as a pastor. During the first year at seminary, Timothy David, their first child, was born but lived only three days. It was a devastating blow to the young couple.

"Because of my own scarring experiences as a child, I never wanted to have children or be a mother," Margene says. "I felt I didn't know how to be a mother. Then I had four children in five years." During the following years, while Tom went through seminary and into the pastorate of Grand Junction Community Church, Colorado, Margene dealt with difficult pregnancies and the challenge of learning how to be a mother to her growing family.

In 1982, Tom and Margene went with their young family to work in Athens with the Greater Europe Mission where Tom taught in the Bible school and was involved in the extension program. When they returned to the United States in 1986, however, Margene was suffering from digestive problems. She had her gall bladder removed and went back to Greece but the problems persisted. Several surgeries later, doctors finally diagnosed her with pseudo-obstructive disease. At the time there were only 400 other known cases in the United States. In 1989 doctors advised her not to go back to Greece. The Greater Europe Mission asked Tom to be the Training Director for the mission in Chicago and Margene entered a two-year graduate school program in Wheaton College. While abroad she had developed an interest in counseling, particularly among missionaries, and as soon as she received her Masters degree in clinical psychology, she pursued her idea of counseling those who were working overseas.

She did all this, however, struggling with her health. Eventually she had to receive all her nourishment through an intravenous tube. Treatment took twelve hours at a time and cost $200 per day. This continued for seven years, during which she was often very ill with infections. When she was well, she would cook for the family, although it was difficult to know what to cook them. "I wasn't hungry myself and I wouldn't be eating the meal with them so I needed them to tell me what I should cook." Longing to be able to live more normally, she put her name on the list for an intestinal transplant, her only hope of being able to eat again. It was three years before her name came up.

On the night before the transplant, Margene and Tom arrived at the hospital around midnight to the strains of "How Great Thou Art" on the car radio. "It was as if the Lord put his arms around us and reminded us that he was in control. It gave me tremendous peace," says Margene. At 7.00 a.m. the next morning, she was wheeled into theatre. It took doctors four and a half hours to remove her small intestine and eight hours to replace it with the donated organ, a very experimental operation as she was the first person ever to receive a small intestine transplant at Northwestern Hospital in Chicago. Five weeks after the surgery, she returned home to celebrate a heartfelt Thanksgiving with her family.

Recovery was not plain sailing, however. Haemorrhaging, organ rejection, and other complications meant that Margene was back in hospital time after time. She suffered from meningitis, pancreatitis, and pneumonia. She spent 150 days of the second year back in hospital and at one stage the doctors even wanted to remove the transplanted organ. At that point Margene's church held a special twenty-four hours of prayer for her. When the doctor saw her next he said, "I don't know what has happened, but you're getting better." Finally, eighteen months after the transplant, Margene began to eat food again for the first time. At first, after not eating for seven years, her taste was so sensitive that everything seemed really strong, either extremely salty or extremely sweet and it took time to adjust. It brought home to her the truth of the verse in Psalm 34:8: "Taste and see that the LORD is good." "Food reminds me of the goodness of God to us which we only understand as we get to know him. The more we experience him in our lives, the more we realize the great things he has in store for us."

Looking back now, Margene is philosophical about all that she went through in the course of the operation and the stressful uncertainty as to its outcome. "I just kept focusing on how different life would be when I was well again and able to live a more normal life" she says. Loving support from her husband, family and church were invaluable but could not prevent occasional low moments during the protracted recovery period following the transplant. When she was tempted to give up hope, she was most aware of God's presence and strength, carrying her through the day and giving her a strong sense that he still had a future for her.

Margene's transplant operation took place in October 1996. The following May, when she was still coping with the post transplant complications, she received another chilling diagnosis—breast cancer. She had a mastectomy but could have no other treatment because of the transplant. She took it all in her stride. "I didn't think of the mastectomy as an issue—it was insignificant compared to the transplant," she says. Then in 2004, she discovered a lump in her other breast.

"God had prepared me," she acknowledges. "I had total peace when the doctor came in and told me it was malignant. Neither Tom nor I were really surprised. Of course we were upset to know the cancer had come back, but we still believed that God was in control."

In recent months, Margene has had fluid removed from her lung and is on oxygen most of the time. She has had eight weeks of hormone treatment but has been told that she cannot have any more. "Again the Lord prepared us," she says. "I cried in the doctor's office when he told me. It is hard, but I have been preparing for this for a long time." Looking back over her life, Margene says that there have been many times when she has been so sick that death seemed imminent and there was no reason that she should survive, but God did not choose to take her at those times. Many times when her youngest daughter, Tirzah, came home from school, she did not know if her mother would be at home or in hospital, feeling well or even dead. So now Margene is content to leave her future in God's hands, knowing that he will not take her until the time is right.

Her friends have rallied round in an amazing way. Some weeks before my visit they brought her a "Blessings Basket." She pointed out to me a basket of beautifully wrapped presents sitting in the corner of the living room. On each present was a gift tag with a verse from the Bible. On one was written simply "God keeps His promises." Her friends left the basket with instructions that she was to open a present anytime she was having a hard day. One day recently when Tom asked her why she had not opened any of the presents she told him, "I haven't had a bad day yet!" She eventually gave in and opened one just to please him because he was anxious to know what the parcels contained. With a smile she showed me the present—a beautiful picture with an inspirational thought that lifts her spirits every time she sees it.

Some friends also organized a "Bless Margene Brunch" where ten of them got together and each brought a special Bible verse to share with her. They laughed and talked, prayed and cried a little, but mostly they praised God together for all his goodness. The organizer was overwhelmed with people who wanted to be part of the event, but she limited the numbers to keep it personal. She had to organize another event for those unable to attend the first one.

Margene is still counseling others, as she is able. "The Lord has given me the strength for the things he has wanted me to do. I feel the counseling of missionaries is so important. If they can receive it both before they go overseas and also while they are there, in order to enable them to stay there, it is a huge blessing. This is what I want to do." She works as a counselor with Greater Europe Mission personnel and managed to travel to Budapest recently for the annual conference where she was able to counsel missionaries who came to the conference from many parts of Europe. In her spare time she is also making personal gifts for her two girls and her son, things that will be meaningful to them when she is gone.

"We do not live as those without hope," she says. "All of us know our days are numbered—mine are probably just less than some others. I think of all those who have blessed me over the years and some of them are with Jesus now. When we are united in heaven it will be as if there has been no passage of time, as if the separation had not happened. Life has been so good that I don't want to swap places with anyone. It is hard to imagine how heaven will be so much better. The only thing that is difficult is watching the family suffer because of me.

"I have had problems eating for many years, but one day soon I will eat at the banqueting table of the Lord. My good friend Carol bought me a copy of the Bible that you read through in a year and there are sweet messages in it for me every day. But I don't know why I'm so particular about keeping to the set passages for each day, because I'll see him before I finish it."

Margene recently received an email from a missionary friend who had been in an intensely bombed area of the Middle East some years ago. She said that at that time when she knew her life could end at any moment she felt an incredible closeness to God. She also said that now she sometimes wishes she could go back to that time because she felt so at peace and so close to him. "I can understand what she means because that is what I am experiencing now," comments Margene.

Margene and Auntie Jean both inspire me as I think about my own life. I want to be like them when I reach the final stage—having a faith that has grown stronger not weaker with the passage of time. Like them, I want to be able to look forward knowing that what appears to be the final stage here is actually the beginning of a whole new adventure, of which we only have brief glimpses and a limited understanding.

When Paul wrote his first letter to the Thessalonians, he encouraged them to live to please God, and to look forward to meeting him face to face. "… And so we will be with the Lord for ever. Therefore encourage each other with these words" (1Thess. 4:17,18). Death is not the end, but a beginning. At the end of *The Last Battle*,[11] C.S. Lewis describes this perfectly as the beginning of the holidays after the end of term, the morning that comes when the dream has ended.

In the meantime, those who have reached this stage before us continue to encourage and inspire us. We can look forward with hope, not dread. God always has new things in store for us, new things to teach us, new ways in which he can use us if we continue to be open to his working in our lives. The important thing today, in whatever season of life we are, is to make sure that no sin is allowed to block our ever-growing, closer relationship with God, to make ourselves completely available to him, to allow him to do what he wants to do in our lives, so that we are ready to face the next stage with our confidence firmly in him. We do not always receive warning before we move from one season of life to the next. Sometimes we are catapulted forward before we know it. But God knows. Let us aim to live so close to him that we are prepared beforehand for whatever comes and are enabled to help others around us to finish well.

**To him who is able to keep you from falling
and to present you before his glorious presence without
fault and with great joy
Jude 24**

Endnotes

1 Lewis Carroll, *Alice in Wonderland* (London: MacMillan, 1865).
2 Michael Griffiths, *Take My Life* (Nottingham, UK: IVP, 1967).
3 J.B. Phillips, *Your God is Too Small* (London: Epworth Press, 1952).
4 Mitch Albom, *Tuesdays with Morrie* (London: Time Warner Books, 1997).
5 E.T. Kramp, D. Kramp, E.P. Mckhann, *Living with the End in Mind* (New York: Three Rivers Press, 1998).
6 "I Love You Lord" by Laurie Klein © 1978, 1980 House of Mercy Music. Admin. by Maranatha! Music.
7 Ruth Fowke, *Personality and Prayer* (Surrey, UK: Eagle, 1997).
8 Thinkexist.com. Permission has been requested.
9 Thinkexist.com. Permission has been requested.
10 Quote from blog. "Emilie Barnes writes in her book, The Spirit of *Loveliness* about a woman that she knew. Her name is Bonnie Green. Here is the excerpt that she especially loves. 'It is the glow within that creates beauty. People are like stained-glass windows. They sparkle like crystal in the sun. At night they continue to sparkle only if there is light from within.'" http://flipflopfloozie.blogspot.com/2005_09_01_archive.html.
11 C.S. Lewis, *The Last Battle* (London: HarperCollins, 1957).